RADICAL VEGETARIANISM

Radical Vegetarianism
A Dialectic of Diet and Ethic

Mark Mathew Braunstein

Panjandrum Books
Los Angeles

Third Printing: 1988

Cover design by Catherine Conner, Oakland, CA.

Library of Congress Cataloging in Publication Data

Braunstein, Mark Mathew, 1951–
    Radical Vegetarianism.

        Bibliography: p. 136
        1. Vegetarianism. 1. Title
TX392.B72   613.2'62'01   81-4724
ISBN 0-915572-52-4   AACR2
ISBN 0-915572-37-0 (pbk.)

For further information:
Panjandrum Books
11321 Iowa Avenue, Suite 1
Los Angeles, Calif. 90025

Manufactured in the United States of America

Contents

II. Ethic

TO

my father
for encouraging my inquiries in
nature

my mother
for feeding my interest in
food

the Daniels and the Davidsons
for nourishing my avocation in the
food of nature

the animals
for guiding my concern in the
nature of food

most especially:
the Dodo
the Passenger Pigeon
the Buffalo

And also much Cattle

I was very sad to hear
that a young buffalo
friend
had recently died

he was buried
at the A & P

Joe Ribar, *The Book of the Buffalo*

*   *   *

You catch a fish. It looks
up at you. You say,
"How beautiful you are, but this
is the worst day of your life."

Norman MacAfee, *12 Nightingales*

Introduction

It is with great excitement and admiration that I share my feelings and thoughts about this book and its overall perspective of the vegetarian movement. Mark is unique in his contribution to the vegetarian literature. *Radical Vegetarianism* blends his expertise in culture, art, science, and in-depth sensitivity to and experience with the many conflicting as well as complementary schools of vegetarian philosophy. Flooded by enthusiasm, I express my feelings for its greatness. But the book offers beyond what I can summarize in brief sketches.

A view of vegetarianism that breaks traditions, this work is a historic perspective that shocks the addictive logic of carnivorous mentality as well as the green underthoughts of the vegetarians whose brains are glued-out on casein and gluten, the white stuff that is as bad as heroin. This book is a labyrinth of thought models within a framework of relevant reverence tied together in a nerve matrix of a carnivorous city of confusion.

His work makes visible the divine architect and the light beams of truth that hold the planet and cosmos together. This book will hang in even after the pages are closed and forgotten.

Mark gives the reader an overview of the dietary myths and heroes filled with humor, irony, sadness, love, and life of the contemporary society. A classic of spiritual dietary parables and riddles, it is a close look into the heart of life.

Based on the many years I have spent in research on and study of the subject of healing, I feel the following guidelines are consistent with and summarize a philosophy of a healing diet so clearly expressed in Mark's book.

Today diet is becoming the way to be Re(sun god)born. We must be born in new true sunlight. Most die from wrong diet. To be made new, one must be reborn in the light of sun-diet.

The Ancients divided dietary produce into four categories:

1. *Purna Amrit Ann* (Rejuvenating) are complete foods rich in all the life-giving dietary factors, such as the eight essential amino acids, supportive fatty acids, varieties of sugars, chelated minerals, enzymes, vitamins, chlorophyll, nucleic acids, hormones, water, and fiber. They have the capacity to make sick old

cells into vital youthful ones, to actualize optimal mental potential, to give psychic gifts, and to assure survival. Sprout mixtures of the tender legumes and grains, and immature greens and grasses, are foods of such caliber.

2. *Sattvic* (Sustaining) foods include juicy, soothing, live, fresh, and agreeable produce. They increase vital force, energy, strength, and health when eaten in moderation. Such foods are raw fruits, succulent vegetables, frugal quantities of seed yogurt, fresh juices, the tender shoot base of mature grasses, mild land weeds, distilled water rejuvelac, and all the foods included in the Purna Amrit category. They can maintain a superior state of health when served plain or in simple mixtures. They give peace of mind and the physical energy to pursue the higher states of consciousness.

3. *Rajasic* (Enervating) foods can be violently bitter, sour, salty, hot, acid, burning, heavy, mucus-forming, and often murky and lacking in brilliant rainbows of colors, especially if prepared by an unloving chef. Frozen and cooked food from non-animal sources, unsprouted grains, unripe and overripe fruits, raw olive oil, raw dairy products, vitamin and synthetic supplements, natural stimulants, non-therapeutic usage of herbs, washed sea weeds, excessive usage of concentrated foods or complex mixtures of avocado, banana, nuts, seeds, brewers' yeast, dried fruits and honey are examples of such foods and/or dietary practices. When used regularly and predominantly in one's diet, they cause eventual ill health, distemper of the mind, stress, and dis-ease. They eventually slow down the biological processes, leave significant waste, and accelerate aging.

4. *Tamasic* (Poisoning) foods are stale, tasteless, impure, chemicalized, processed, overcooked, or recooked foods. These include animal flesh, fast foods, fried foods, vinegar, bottled oils (other than raw olive—we get more oil than we need in natural, whole foods), canned produce, and white flour bakery products. They have no life in them. As a result, to eliminate them, an enormous amount of life force has to be stolen from the body. Such foods should be avoided.

In this age of pollution and questionable foods sources, of not-so-fresh and all-too-expensive organic produce, we can all benefit highly by including an abundant supply of the inexpensive Rejuvenating foods in our diets.

The individual should *gradually* make dietary changes by reducing and eventually eliminating intake of all Poisoning foods, cutting down on Enervating foods, and increasing an emphasis on Rejuvenating and Sustaining foods. *Do not rush.*

For the highly disciplined who are at peace with themselves and aiming for highest consciousness, or the sick under the guidance of someone of experience in a healing program and associated elimination practices, a diet of a minimum of sixty percent Rejuvenating and the remaining Sustaining foods, with lots of juices, should be followed.

For the individual who lives "in the world" and leads a physically active life, fifty percent Rejuvenating, thirty percent Sustaining, and twenty percent Enervating foods is feasible.

One should realize there is no perfect diet for all times for an evolving, or fully evolved, conscious body.

The most important dietary guidelines are: consistency; slow change guided by dictates of the body; eating whole, natural foods; eating frugally, only when hungry; chewing food until liquid; cutting down protein intake; and eliminating all concentrated cooked protein food. During transition into raw foods and/or for "normal-balance-lifestyle," using baked/steamed roots (carrot, sweet potato, onion . . .) and hard vegetables (cauliflower, broccoli, winter squashes . . .), dried or toasted essene bread, soaked and then low-heat cooked grains, is a way of keeping one's Rajasic body from becoming overwhelmingly Tamasic from released cell garbage, as it is becoming Sattvic through a gentle cleansing program.

One of the gravest sins folks make is to strive toward becoming fruitarian, liquidarian, or breatharian. The only ones who have achieved and maintain such regimens are those who have found such diets necessary for their spiritual level of consciousness. They needed these diets and they felt comfortable with them. Folks who force themselves to do some special diet trip—often motivated by ego and the desire for powers—fail. They vacillate between extremes. They "food trip" for a few days to several months on raw foods and juices, then follow this by feasts of gluttony on cake, ice cream, and pizza.

As some last thoughts, with the new age being flooded by money-hungry charlatans and fools in the health field claiming to be spiritualized holistic doctors and charging outrageous consultation fees for devastating practices—Beware. All is not well in their offices. Read good books for perspective: Brother Mark's, Dr. Ann Wigmore's, Dr. Christopher's, Professor Ehret's, and Dr. Shelton's works. They can save many hundreds of dollars of worthless advice.

Do not be conned into believing you need daily to eat "kooked" food (which will eventually make you kooky)—1 pound of tofu, ½ pound of rice, cow's milk yogurt, vitamins D & B12 supplements, bread—just to be a healthy vegetarian. Mark's book will give you the vision of truth applied to the madness of modern times.

This book is relevant to all brothers and sisters as well as to the lives of our animal friends. It helps us to see more clearly and to become more honest in all our relationships with all life forms. I love you Mark for serving us such a literary delicacy that can be enjoyed without dessert. The book is not radical, only its readers.

VIKTORAS KULVINSKAS, M.S.
Author of *Survival into the 21st Century* and *Sprout for the Love of Everybody.*

Director, Survival Foundation, Inc.

(free information center)
Woodstock Valley, CT 06282

Prelusive Parable

My discourse does not bring with it an exhortation to every description of men. For it is not directed to those who are occupied in sordid mechanical arts, nor to those who are engaged in athletic exercises; neither to soldiers, nor sailors, nor rhetoricians, nor to those who lead an active life. But I write to the man who considers what he is, whence he came, and whither he ought to tend, and who, in what pertains to nutriment, and other necessary concerns, is different from those who propose to themselves other kinds of life; for to none but such as these do I direct my discourse.

> PORPHYRY
> *On Abstinence*
> *From Animal Food*, Book I,
> Section 27

We understand a thought the way we digest food, so those of us whose minds are in our stomachs had best learn to keep our mouths shut. "Jaisa khaye ann, taisa hove mann," a Hindustani proverb goes: "You are what you eat." But you are also why you eat. That England is notorious for unsavory cuisine and is also renowned for animal protection, anti-vivisectionism, and vegetarianism is no mere coincidence.

What I have written here is not just a book to convert carnivores to vegetarianism—for we have enough of those, and besides the majority of readers on vegetarianism already are vegetarians—but a polemic to persuade ethical vegetarians of the moral necessity of health and to convince those concerned only with nutrition to consider also the unhealthy consequences of perdition.

Between the many questions of philosophies and the few answers of recipes, between the religious and the delicious, we slice our fruits and vegetables along the sharp edge between life and death. For these are our subjects: not just fruits and vegetables, but life and death. Whether it is easier to get to the mind inside the body through the body, or to the body inside the mind through the mind, is a riddle as yet unsolved. Either way the two are inseparable; if the external is not pure then neither can the internal be so.

The odor of the breath might be checked by holding hand to mouth and quickly inhaling through the nose after slowly exhaling; but if the hand itself reeks, we can never know the source of the foulness. Once aspiring to be a painter and a poet, I abandoned murals for morals and poetics for polemics. We first must wash our hands of blood before staining them again with paint and ink.

M.M.B.
New York City
September, 1980

I. Diet

You can believe me or not as you like; but truths are not such tough old Methuselahs as most people imagine. A normal, ordinary truth is good for, say, seventeen or eighteen—at most twenty years; seldom more. And truths as venerable as that are nothing but skin and bones; yet it isn't until then that the great majority adopts them and prescribes them to Society as wholesome spiritual food. But there's not much nourishment in that kind of diet, I assure you; as a doctor you can take my word for that. These tired old truths are as rancid and moldy as last year's bacon; they're the cause of all that moral scurvy that plagues Society.

HENRIK IBSEN
An Enemy of the People

1. Nutrition in the Light of Vegetarianism

The popular medical formulation of morality that goes back to Ariston of Chios, "virtue is the health of the soul," would have to be changed to become useful, at least to read: "your virtue is the health of your soul." For there is no health as such, and all attempts to define a thing that way have been wretched failures. Even the determination of what is healthy for your body depends on your goal, your horizon, your energies, your impulses, your errors, and above all on the ideals and the phantasms of your soul. Thus there are innumerable healths of the body; and the more we allow the unique and incomparable to raise its head again, and the more we abjure the dogma of the "equality of men," the more must the concept of a normal *health, along with a* normal *diet and the* normal *course of an illness, be abandoned by medical men. Only then would the time have come to reflect on the health and illness of the soul, and to find the peculiar virtue of each man in the health of his soul. In one person, of course, this health could look like its opposite in another person.*

FRIEDRICH NIETZSCHE
The Gay Science, Book III
Number 120

' 'What must we eat so that we are not merely the product of what we eat?'' asks Rudolf Steiner in a lecture entitled ''Nutritional Questions in the Light of Spiritual Science,'' translated as ''Problems of Nutrition,'' but which simply could have been called ''Problems.'' ''What It Means to Be a Vegetarian'' could be the title of our book at hand, and ''What It Means to Be Healthy'' and ''What It Means to Be Moral'' could be its two halves' subtitles. In the end, what we are really concerned about is ''Moral Health'' or ''Health of the Soul.'' But this is only the beginning.

Every ethnic group possesses its own foods, and often its own diseases. Thus for supervision in these matters we can no longer look to our parents. Nor can we look to our friends who, in one breath apologize for the flesh on their plates, yet in the next breath swallow it. Sometimes they eat faster in the presence of

3

vegetarians, as though wishing to end the subject as quickly as possible. Nor can we look to animals. Though we look like apes, we do not live like apes, so we cannot eat like apes. Even two apes eat differently from each other if one lives in an African jungle, while the other dwells in an American zoo. If we were to imitate either's diet, it would have to be that of the latter, the prisoner behind bars.

Some might consider any emphasis on food completely irrelevant: the person who eats beer and franks with cheer and thanks might just happen to live longer than someone who eats pears and flax with fear and angst.

Health, however, is not merely long life, but also complete freedom from disease, no matter how long or short the life. One who lives for fifty years in good health with the least possible sleep has already lived longer than one in ill health for seventy-five years, much of it in pain and most of it in bed. Swift describes in *Gulliver's Travels* the immortal Struldbruggs of the land of the Luggnaggians who were doomed to eternal senility since they could not die. Apollo granted the Sibyl of Cumae life for as many grains of sand as she held in her hand. But she was not so wise in her youth as when Aeneas met her seven hundred years later, for she had neglected to ask for beauty and health along with immortality. "I want to die," she told the hero.

The best possible nutrition alone cannot insure the best possible health, nor does the worst sort of food distinctively cause the worst health. Nevertheless, the major cause of illness is poor nutrition. Samuel Butler describes in *Erewhon* a utopian society where the sick are put in jails, not hospitals, since sickness is a crime as much against humanity as against the hindered individual. Disease is not some sin for which one is punished, but is itself the punishment for another sin. Poor nutrition is the sin; poor health is consequently the punishment.

Civilization's last hope of survival rests on every individual's first hope: proper nutrition. In Germany today, as in Erewhon, the sick are sent to the reform house, *reformhaus* meaning in German the "health food store." In England today, users of heroin—white and refined much like flour, sugar, salt and baking powder—are hospitalized. Yet hospitalization is not without risks, for an examination of patients' meals shows that dieticians are as ill-informed as most patients. There too is the domain of doctors of medicine, which is to say doctors of disease, since medicine is a science concerned only with regaining, not maintaining, health.

Donors are advised by doctors neither to smoke tobacco nor to drink alcohol for one hour after giving blood, and before departure from the lab are given coffee and donuts. Were the doctors as much concerned with body types as with blood types, they would advise never to smoke or drink and would instead provide a piece of fruit. Who is still fool enough to take seriously modern medicine's advice in matters of health, and therefore of life and death? Those defrauded by Western nutrition the first half of their lives are destined to be victimized by Western medicine the second half.

State sales taxes are often levied upon all but the very essential. Thus in some states food and drugs are defined as such absolute necessities, while in others only the drugs go untaxed. Official dogma would have us believe it is more important to cure a disease than to prevent it, and that drugs are more sustaining than food. Those who know things better rather than backwards are as suspicious of the AMA as of the FDA.

No medicine has ever cured the body of a disease, but then neither has any food; rather, the body cures itself. All that a medicine or food can do is help the body to help itself. Better to depend on food, the twice or thrice-daily answer to the constant question the body poses. Magnesium, calcium and the rest of the nutrients essential to life, if isolated as pills in a chemically pure form cannot sustain life in any animal. They must be fed as found in food. Food in a highly refined form, devoid of elements naturally inherent in it, also barely sustains life. Life depends not on mere chart values found in books, but rather on intrinsic organic energy which unites a living cell with its elements, making it more than the sum of its parts. This "more" is the life force.

Nutritionists make claims about the nutritional equivalency of pills with food, but never speak about the spiritual. This spirit is impossible to define; it is, by nature, unnameable, ineffable. It plumbs depths which the eye never sees and which the intellect senses only obliquely, yet its effects are as apparent as the look on a face. Experienced health food salespeople know by that look whether a customer has come to purchase food or vitamin pills.

We must learn to eat with judgment, to digest with deliberation. By at all times eating the right food—and at the right times eating no food—the body will expel accumulated toxins. Ultimately and endlessly, eating requires as much care and intelligence as reading. Instead of reading *War and Peace*, some save time and read a synopsis. Likewise, instead of eating real food, some follow the American tradition of popping pills. Vitamins are at best a supplement, never a substitute. Similarly, no one who reads a synopsis can hope to experience the revelations and frustrations of Pierre, Natasha, and Prince Andrei.

All through life we read books and eat food. Early in life we should read books about eating food. We need invest only half a year searching for a suitable system of nutrition to be repaid a dividend of half a lifetime at maturation. But study as we may, we must remember that what one nutritionist writes is right for one person only; that nutritionist. No reader should follow a diet because an author follows it (if, indeed, the author follows it). Rather, students should read a hundred books and formulate one plan from them, just as each author had done in reading a thousand books, devising ten diets, and writing one book. In the end, though, every diet is wrong. No matter what we eat, we die. Thus, that system which promotes the longest life is merely the least wrong.

Where neophyte vegetarians go wrong nutritionally is not in having omitted flesh, but in continuing to eat everything else as before without care of substitution for the omission. Their unhealthiness stands as an example for carnivores to point to in rationalizing their diets. (The common practice of exhibiting the unhealthiest specimens of the different regimens as standards is equivalent to establishing rules through their exceptions.) Consider the classic plastic fast-food meal of hamburger, french fries, Coke and pie. Never mind that the potatoes are fried in left-over hamburger fat, that the Coke contains sugar whose refining uses animal bone, that the pie crust is often made with animal shortening. Eliminate the burger and the diner is deprived of the one vestige of nutrition in the meal; if the meal minus the meat is still eaten, its constant repetition can only cause degeneration into sickness. Though healthy vegetarians are generally healthier than healthy carnivores, unhealthy vegetarians generally are unhealthier. The one step of leaving out flesh is not a deed which makes any future act superior. The average vegetarian must possess a little more than average knowledge about nutrition.

If we have abandoned flesh eating so that others might find

more on the bones they pick, we must still investigate nutrition and, in the process, abandon garbage-eating: white flour, white sugar, white shortening, white baking powder, white salt, white milk (what a delicious cake!) and so on down the line of what should be whitewashed down the drain. As important as knowing what to eat is knowing what not to eat. Early in grade school, children are taught the four basic food groups: meat, poultry, and fish; eggs, milk, and dairy products; fruits and vegetables; and nuts, seeds and grains. Our teachers said we needed a daily selection from each group, and being children we believed them. But now that we are too old to be their students we realize that they were too foolish to have been our teachers. What they called nutrition, we now call gluttony.

Where there is no choice, there is no sacrifice. Some would as readily eat monkey meat if it were made available in their markets, or cat flesh if it became common, as they do their legs of lamb and calf cutlets. That the apes live so near to us on the evolutionary ladder is not the only reason they do not find their way into culinary ladles; rather, with so many ending on laboratory tables, hardly enough are left for butcher blocks. And because dogs and cats play next door is not why they do not end in our next meal; rather, they too eat flesh, so their own does not taste as good as the vegetarian farm and fish animals they are given to eat. Obviously, people eat not so much out of choice as out of convenience.

American carnivorism fits right in with American consumerism, and it is the American way of eating with which we are specifically concerned. Differences exist in carnivorism between one geographic/economic area and another. For instance, Asia differs so greatly from America that the question should be considered whether the same term should even apply to both. The point is that an Asian carnivore shares more in common with an American vegetarian than with an American carnivore. Most Europeans eat flesh frequently but not heavily, sprinkling specks here and there into their grains and into their vegetables; but Americans, Australians and Argentinians—the people of the three great cattle countries—eat grains and vegetables mostly as side dishes.

The typical American carnivore consumes flesh at least once a day and as much as once a meal; whereas the average Asian indulges no more than once a week, maybe once a month, and in fish flesh and sea meats at that. Few national cuisines emphasize the ingredient of flesh so obsessively as ours. Thus, the carnivorism referred to henceforth shall be the middle-class American type, both because of its extreme example and its particular relevance.

Carnivores can be healthy, and health itself is important, but more important is its attainment at the least effort and expense. For true health is maintained not by the development of will power but by the elimination of inessentials. If good health can be gained from elimination of one food group, namely pieces of dead animals (meat, poultry, fish and sea meats), then maybe better health could come from eliminating another group, namely products of live animals (eggs, milk and dairy).

"Baloney!" the reader might gasp, but the Five Books of Moses admonishes us not to cook a kid in its mother's milk, a kind of respect for the dead but not yet buried. Kosher and other Semitic dietary laws prohibiting the mixing of meat and milk imply the inadvisability of each alone, like alcohol and barbiturates (but not like fruits and vegetables, which one should eat, but not together). Perhaps the analogy totters on the tenuous. If so, it is only an affirmation of its worthiness of consideration. So long as we do not forget that a book read is not a life led, those nutritionists—whether self-declared or college-degreed—whose views are shocking, who demand what appears difficult, are precisely the ones worth reading. That something is difficult might be more reason to do it. After all, vegetarianism is difficult, but only within the confines of a carnivorous society, and then only at first, like fasting: the fast the first day, vegetarianism the first year. Nutrition and health writers who do not condemn cadaver consumption may be hesitant about asking the difficult of themselves and their readership, since they are writing commercially for large audiences.

Most diet authors say next to nothing about carnivorism, and nothing about vegetarianism. And some say less than nothing or, worse, they condemn vegetarianism. Oriented toward the easy out, they are well rewarded for their orthodox views. Jean Mayer, when seated sweetly on his chair at Harvard, endowed by the sugar industry, suggested that strict vegetarianism may stem from a "deep-seated psychological difficulty"[1] and advised parents of children who will not eat meat to seek the services not of the school nutritionist but of the school psychiatrist.

Carlton Fredericks—quick to recommend his radio show advertisers and lethargic about mentioning the products of anyone

---

1. Jean Mayer, *A Diet for Living*, p. 184.

else—labels vegetarianism a "cult" that "represents more of a neurosis than a credo," and then asks: "Why avoid meat when a cow is merely walking grass?"[2] For that matter, "All flesh is grass" (Isaiah 40:6). Maybe a cow *is* walking grass. Let it walk. Let it walk of its own accord to its grave in the grass.

A cow would be nothing more than walking grass were it not for the cow spirit about her, just as Mr. Fredericks would be nothing more than a writing cow were it not for the human spirit about him. But ours is a materialistic society which places no value in spiritual matters because these cannot be bottled and bought. That is the spirit's great fortune.

Still, all these words are but pointers to the way, not the way itself. Even *if* vegetarianism were proven unhealthy, those vegetarians concerned with matters beyond health would nevertheless refuse to feed their children animals and animal products, since animals too are someone's children.

But ours is a free as well as a materialistic society, where angels of the spirit can battle with books against materialists as vegetarians can speak against carnivores. For vegetarianism, Walker, Lust, Shelton, Kulvinskas, Kirschner, Warmbrand, Bircher-Benner, Wigmore, Ohsawa, Ehret, and Airola are eloquent spokespersons. Paul Bragg too can be considered a vegetarian; he ate flesh whenever he wished . . . about once every ten years. (Was he really writing a book entitled "I Challenge Death" when, at the age of ninety-five, he died?) Each presents a system of vegetarian health, none necessarily better than the other and each unique. Though confusion might arise out of the diversity, many systems work, indeed any system works—an affirmation of the wonders of both the human body and the whole of nature.

All the above agree upon abstinence from flesh, and all but one upon abstinence from pills. Indeed, even the father of Western medicine, Hippocrates, advised us to leave drugs in the chemist's pot if we can be healed by food; so we first must know what is the right food. We need not know any system; knowing what is the right food is enough. For instance, George Ohsawa's macrobiotics prescribes mostly cooked grains and beans and proscribes most fruits; whereas Herbert Shelton's natural hygiene prescribes mostly raw vegetables and raw fruits and proscribes all cooked grains and beans. Although opposite theories, each works for different people. (A defense of macrobiotics, less the salt and cooked vegetables, is perhaps warranted due to the cry of carnivorous

---

2. Carlton Fredericks, *The Nutrition Handbook*, p. 142.

wolf from Jean Mayer and his flock, but is not the main matter here.) For the only one who should sternly follow Ohsawa's system is Ohsawa, or Shelton's system is Shelton; for their readers, eclecticism, not epigonism, should be the rule.

One reader might combine the two systems; that is, he eats mostly raw fruits and raw nuts and some raw vegetables during the summer, and mostly cooked grains and cooked beans with some cooked vegetables during the winter. Spring and fall are periods of transition as much for him as for the plants he eats. He aspires to a diet solely of fruits and nuts and sea vegetables: that which grows on the tops of trees and on the bottoms of seas, both the highest and lowest forms of vegetable life. All he or anyone might wish of vegetarianism in purely personal terms is that it promote a long, healthful life.

The description of real life as healthy life may be inadequate, but that of "health foods" as real foods is not. Some view "real foods" enthusiasts as selfish fetishists, not just concerned with their health but concerned *only* with their health; it is, however, at least as selfish and far more wasteful to seek a cure for sickness derived from long years of eating fake foods. Furthermore, some complain that "real foods" do not taste good. But how could they know, when their bodies and sense organs have been desensitized by the consumption of meat and spicy foods (and, perhaps, alcohol and tobacco as well)?

Any food tastes better than aspirin and penicillin. Americans consume more meat and medication than any other population, for the practice of flesh eating goes hand in hand with pill popping. The food in our life is beneficial only as long as there is life in our food. A vitamin pill, synthetic or natural, may be identical to that vitamin as found in real food, but it is only one element and does little good if not combined with other nutrients.

Another misconception concerning real food is that, tasty or not, it hardly satisfies the appetite—an apparent cause of slimness among its adherents. Actually a slice of white bread supplies so little nutrition that the diner is forced to consume four or five slices where one slice of whole grain would suffice. Hence obesity is itself a sickness, a sort of "sufficiency disease:" fat people may be compared with their white bread, inflated receptacles of vacuity.

There are many kinds of healthy people, many kinds of health, many kinds of ill people, but only a few kinds of illnesses: besides hereditary disease, most illness is deficiency disease. But even those illnesses of our ancestors may be linked to food and drink, since we tend to eat the same as they did. Modern medicine reflects modern materialism since it attributes diseases of the body to the presence of something from without, not the absence of something within.

We might worry that eating only real food does not supply the necessary nutrients, perhaps because of modern methods of chemical fertilization and prolonged refrigeration. But we need worry more for other reasons: what suffers most from the artificiality of modern technology is not our food but our lives. We must truly earn our food not with mere money but with sweat, for to eat enough to insure salubrity without obesity we must engage in adequate exercise. This could mean an early morning jog around a few blocks. One reason Americans most often exercise early in the morning is that it is the only time their stomachs are empty. To be able to exercise enough we must eat only those foods which do not weigh us down, thus eschewing fatty flesh food. If we are unable to dash away from the table after a meal, we should not have sat down in the first place. The average vegetarian is two to ten kilograms lighter than the average carnivore, and the average carnivore is just as much overweight—a statistic which affirms not the health of the vegetarians, but the ill health of the carnivores. If we as vegetarians eat less, we still are eating as much as we want of all we want; a healthy person neither needs nor wants too much food.

Good nutrition is only a few rungs up the ladder from bad nutrition. The ladder has no end, at least it is not within sight as we stumble up each rung: we do not climb into a healthy body and just stay there; we go through it, come out the other side into a healthy mind, and in time unite the two into a healthy spirit. This is not to say the spirit cannot develop ahead of both mind and body; often it does, only its task is more difficult. Thus with no regard for the healthful aspects of animal abstinence, we might help the body along in spite of itself and be vegetarians out of a more metaphysical motive.

Big fish kill small fish, small people kill big and small fish, and big people kill big fish, small fish, small people and themselves. Who but the biggest of all big people can hope to restrain any of this killing; and how but by killing can anyone hope to enforce it? As an answer to such questions, vegetarianism embodies religion, as many religions embody vegetarianism. But unlike religious prohibitions, the compulsion for vegetarianism must come from within. One should no more compel another to eat one's food than to be oneself, for one's food is oneself. Not everyone was meant to be a vegetarian.

Every human might be identified with an entire species of animals. Indeed, as many different types of humans exist as there are distinct animal species. Thus, some humans resemble herbivorous chipmunks, deer, or giraffes; others vegetarian hogs, elephants, or hippopotami; still others carnivorous tigers, wolves, or vultures. As is true in the animal kingdom, most humans eat no flesh at all or at most once a week. The point is that if many of us are meant to eat as the apes do, some of us are meant to eat as the lions do. But the ratio of American human carnivore to vegetarian is far greater than in the animal kingdom. If more lions than zebras roamed the savannas, the lions would eventually wipe out both the zebras and themselves. In essence this is happening to us: too many lions dwell among us in our brutalized, big cities.

Vegetarianism is a diet which offers a panacea for a long life not just for particular humans, but for the race as a whole. Our sophistry cannot escape the justice, unsleeping and unerring, of nature. And yet, and yet: humans do differ from animals; animals are governed by natural law, humans by natural law and by free will. Thus each member of the human family resists nature merely in being human. We are humans, different from other animals; and we are individuals, different from other humans. Along with lists of well-known reasons for vegetarianism, some accumulate lists of well-known vegetarians, presenting that second list as though part of the first. Who should care how many great people have been vegetarians? That many, great or common, have done something is no reason for another's doing it; surely far more great people in Western history have been carnivorous. No list of thousands counts as much as the individual plurality of one; vegetarianism is not in need of credentials, references, or membership lists. The only vegetarian one need know is oneself—as one need know oneself generally.

Minerals are material. Plants are material and alive. Animals are material, alive, and sentient. Higher animals are material, alive, sentient, and mental. Humans are material, alive, sentient, mental, and sentimental. Each evolutionary form incorporates and adds to the form before and below it. Thus each knows not only itself but the form before it on the evolutionary scale, perhaps more of that form than it knows of itself. Except for general habits which might be useful in its capture, a carnivorous animal knows less about its prey's life than a carnivorous human knows about the farm animal. Whereas the animal of prey knows mostly about its victim only during its final hours, the civilized human knows just the opposite, that is, more of its life than of its death.

Vegetarians are not a better sort of people, just a better sort of carnivore; and carnivores are just a better sort of cannibal. On the assumption they would become depositaries of their vanquished enemies' courage and strength, ancient warriors ate the brains, heart, organs, or whole bodies of their conquered. In modern times, human animals no longer eat other humans, even their enemies; but other animals are still eaten as though *they* were enemies. The breeds of animals eaten have changed, however. Past centuries fed heavily on wild animals; the primary source now is domasticated (sic) animals, those changed, and chained, by human will.

Still, the universe manifests its order in a way people who have long lost touch with nature can hardly suspect. We are allotted only a fixed amount of food for our lifetimes: no more, though sometimes less. We also are responsible for the future into which we shall move, sooner or later creating one in which there is no more room to move. Those who eat more than youth's or midlife's share become fat: fat people die young, having exhausted their allowance early. Flesh eaters every year require six hectares of land to feed a cow with grains and grasses that they might feed themselves with beef, as opposed to lacto-vegetarians who ask two hectares to feed a cow grains and grasses that they might feed themselves with milk, as opposed to complete vegetarians who detour the cow altogether and humbly beg but half a hectare to feed themselves with grains and grasses. Conservation of soil, air, water, and plant and animal life in general rests most precariously on the conservation of calories.

But more important than the caloric is the karmic debt. It's bad enough to kill an animal, it 's worse still to raise it precisely to be killed. Life in the darkened veal stall or the cramped battery cage is hardly life at all compared to freedom in the forest. It's bad enough to kill an animal; it's worst of all to eat it. The inherent cholesterol, toxins, uric acid, high bacteria count, general indigestibility, and lack of fiber in the flesh of an animal whose life was aborted in turn shortens the life of the eater animal. "Shortening" is no euphemism for "lard."

Generations ago, when there was more wilderness, eating an animal was not such a malevolent act; wild animals abounded, and fewer people were around to eat them. In the wild, those animals that endured the first weeks after birth lived longer; natural selection discards the very oldest first, the very youngest

second, and all the others third. But factory farming has inter-
fered with nature's designs, and most animals never live past the
time they attain full biological growth. So the debt humans
accumulate increases, repaid by shorter healthy lives. The pen-
alties are enforced by technologies: added antibiotics, sodium
nitrates and nitrites and other preservatives, injected artificial
hormones, and accumulated insecticides in the bodies of the
farm animals. The animals' own hormones, particularly adren-
aline, and unexpelled toxins and wastes are secreted at the
slaughtering places. These poisons serve to shorten and sicken
the lives of those who serve and eat the flesh. Those who live by
the swordfish die by the swordfish.

On evidence as obvious as the omnipresent golden arches
which rise above the highway like Parsee Towers of Silence, an
American carnivore consumes an estimated weight of flesh total-
ing more than half a steer a year. The steer is rare that is allowed
to live longer than two of its otherwise twenty-two years of life,
so a karmic debt of those fifteen to twenty unlived years of a
steer life is accumulated. Accumulated by whom? By the steer's
unknown mother? By its unborn young? By the factory farmer?
By the hot dog vendor on the street? Clearly it is by, more than
any other, the carnivore.

Let us imagine a scale in eternity's ledger whereby the worth
of each species on the earth, indeed, the worth of the earth, is
tabulated. It might reveal that a year of a chicken's life equals a
month of a sheep's equals a week of a cow's equals a day of a
human's. Based on arbitrary assumptions about this hypothetical
golden rule, stolen steer life converts at the exchange rate of one
steer week to one human day. Fifteen stolen steer years times
fifty-two weeks a year yields 780 weeks of steer life, which in
turn equals 780 days of human life—roughly two years. This
two-year "human-steer" debt corresponds exactly to the human
time taken to accumulate it, so each day a person remains a carnivore in his youth represents at the end one less day of good
health, or of life altogether.

This method of calculation is the basis of much criminal sen-
tencing, wherein one year of one human life equals one year of
another human life (an eye for an eye, a tooth for a tooth): third-
degree murderers accumulate debts equal to the duration the deceased might otherwise have lived and, assuming murderer and
murdered are about the same age, often the cases of both best
friends and worst enemies, the criminals are sentenced to life
imprisonment.

Though we are prisoners of our bodies, we have no cause to

suffer our incarceration. When just one passion overcomes the body, it allows easy access to all the rest. The alcoholic and narcotic, the libertine and nicotine, are all habits which combine forces to overwhelm the body and cause it to fall. Those who seek to create harmony out of a carnivorous diet might as well seek peace out of necromancy. Searching is in itself good, but useless when in the wrong place altogether. Better to save time and not seek it; better to save crime and leave it out. Why indenture our souls with bodies of others? Is not our own enough? Is not our own too much? Blacks from Africa traveling in Europe sometimes say they are American. Whites from America traveling in Africa sometimes say they are Canadian. Dare Eskimos traveling in America say they are penguins? Or walruses? Indeed, because they eat them, Eskimos come closer to being walrus than any of the others to those they claim. It's hard enough to be ourselves, we need not try to be cows, pigs, lambs, or walruses.

Certain organs, such as livers and kidneys, filter and accumulate food poisons, including insecticides. What these organs do in human bodies they do also in animal bodies: eating the animal body, particularly its liver, gathers not just the human share but also the animal's. If you are what you eat, it is because you are what you do not excrete. No wonder kidneys are so often overworked in flesh eaters: they must cleanse not just the bodies of the eaters, but the bodies of all those eaten.

It is ridiculous to try to know oneself amidst the confusing presence of so many other bodies within our own. When the tongue must taste another's tongue, the stomach digest another's stomach, the blood vessels circulate another's blood, the intestines excrete as feces another's intestines and feces, who can ''know oneself?'' Rather gnaw oneself.

Time now to progress from commentary to commitment: presentation of these ''problems of nutrition'' is hardly justified without one suggestion of solution. Three rules exist for choosing our food, keys with which to open the door of our own flowering: eat food as raw, as whole, and as unprocessed as possible.

Dare carnivores eat flesh raw, blood still pulsating from uneviscerated bodies? But who objects to an apple just picked from the tree, sap still dripping from the stem? Furthermore, most vegetables that we are used to cooking actually taste better raw, a fact most of us are too habituated to recognize. Raw plant foods retain all their beneficial enzymes, some of which even assist our digestion of those plants; but the only enzymes flesh contains are the ones we would not want, those which in larger amounts would digest us. When a human eats tongue, who is tasting whom? Food should be eaten raw whenever possible; flesh, on the other hand, *must* be cooked to destroy all its germs.

Second, concerning whole foods, few animals are eaten entirely in one sitting. Six or seven sardines might be swallowed in one sandwich, but two years are needed to consume the equivalent of one steer. This is only statistical since most shy away from organs, eating them only when disguised inside intestinal casings and called cold cuts and hot dogs: if these eaters knew they were eating brains and eyes, perhaps their brains would guide them where their eyes had failed. Everything in nature harmonizes both with nature and to itself. The term "natural" applies to those foods that are balanced and that maintain harmony within their consumers, so that they in turn will do so with the whole of nature. Hence natural food store shelves are nearly fleshless, and one in six such shoppers is vegetarian.

Third, concerning unprocessed foods, no improvement can be made upon nature in the matter of nutrition. Any alteration of food that occurs in the name of preservation or delectation acts only to diminish nutrition. Cooking, for instance, never puts anything in, but only takes away. Often this alteration renders the food unrecognizable, and nearly as often this is done purposely; thus, few can discern the lamb from its chops or the pig from its pork. Flesh is food processed before any human has even seen it: it is recomposed plants hidden behind and inside an animal.

Those who attempt to know the inner self find that a host of deviations, all inimical to progress, appear out of the unknown, or rather out of their own unknowing. It is a long, hard climb for the body up the mountain of the mind. We need be neither orologists nor mountaineers to know that the very dead weight of animals slung across our shoulders or around our bellies hardly assuages the strain of the endeavor. The higher the mountain and the longer the climb, the smaller we then see ourselves to be. Not all religious movements or spiritual leaders proscribe carnivorism, but then almost none explicitly demand it either. Those who have gained self-realization can understand how inconsequential all humanity is, and can know that all its actions, good or bad, real or imagined, intended or accidental, amount either to nothing in the face of loftiness, or perhaps to something infinitely small. Such people commit only those actions which reflect that understanding, actions which in themselves can count like Pascal's wager either for good or for nothing, but never for bad. Such an action is vegetarianism.

2. Ashes to Ashes, Life to Life

I swallow down my food, but the slightest preliminary methodical politico-economical observation of it does not seem to me worthwhile. In this connection the essence of all knowledge is enough for me, the simple rule with which the mother weans the young ones from her teats and sends them out into the world: "Water the ground as much as you can." And in this sentence is not almost everything contained? What has scientific inquiry, ever since our first fathers inaugurated it, of decisive importance to add to this? Mere details, mere details, and how uncertain they are: but this rule will remain as long as we are dogs. It concerns our main staple of food: true, we have also other resources, but only at a pinch, and if the year is not too bad we could live on this main staple of our food; this food we find on the earth, but the earth needs our water to nourish it and only at that price provides us with our food, the emergence of which, however, and this should not be forgotten, can also be hastened by certain spells, songs and ritual movements.

FRANZ KAFKA
"Investigations
of a Dog"

Birth is a miracle, death a mystery, but life need be neither misery nor a mistake. Life can be devoted either to soul or to soma, depending in part on whether the mind is three times a day on sesame seeds and sprouts or all the day on aches and pains. Beginning from the mortal wound of birth, for those whose days are measured by diseases alternating between acute and chronic, life is a long disease cured only and slowly by death, the way a jet high in the stratosphere begins its descent many miles before its destination.

"We shall try to achieve 'ataraxia,' the undisturbed peace of mind before the turmoil of this world," wrote Luigi Cornaro a half millennium ago, quoting a passage Zeno had written a millennium before. The Greek and Italian were separated by more than just the Adriatic and by more than just a thousand years, but mostly by their two opposing views of actual achievement of "ataraxia:" Zeno, the first Stoic, believed all occurrence was the

17

result of divine will and, therefore, we should accept our fates with calm and without complaint, while Cornaro believed we can take our lives into our hands because we, after all, can take our foods into our hands. Cornaro is our first modern writer on nutrition. What he wrote then is no less true now, just as most current writings on nutrition are no different from and nothing newer than what was written in the first American health food books at the beginning of the twentieth century.

Cornaro's youth and middle age were marked by indulgence in all that wealthy Venice offered, funded by what others had earned. At forty he contracted a near-fatal illness, but through a life of simplicity and moderation regained his health and lived to a ripe one hundred and two. During his last sixty years, the author of *La Vita Sobria* redirected his efforts to serving the same people upon whom he was previously parasitic. He became an architect and helped to build Venice. Everything gotten *must* be given back.

Most nutritionists are more akin to mathematicians with tables and charts, and to physicians with tablets and shots, than to metaphysicians. Neither theologicians nor moral philosophers equate health with virtue; neither doctors nor nutritionists associate sickness with sin.

When one thing precedes another their relationship may either be causation or succession. The American diet obviously leads the way to many diseases, but the diet and the diseases could very well stem from a common ground: perdition. In such cases, disease might be not the concern of doctors, but of priests. Christian Scientists partially agree. And we cannot hold our tongues while those who take our pulses also take our purses. The society which permits the sale of alcohol, prescription pills, tobacco, coffee, tea, and flesh is as responsible and condemnable for illnesses as the individual who purchases them.

Economic systems actually stand more to profit or to suffer from an individual's health or illness than any one individual. Declines and falls of civilizations are popularly attributed to mere political or social causes because of an equally prevalent disregard for nutrition, but some historians have attributed Rome's fall less to Attila and more to the opium in the Romans' smoking pipes and to the lead in their water pipes. Nations, like individual citizens, are born, grow, age, and die. Death must be accepted, indeed expected, with life. Food, which is life, whether from plants or from animals from plants, nurtures this process which does not end but is only reprocessed into the same soil from which the plants originally grew. Everything gotten must be given back.

Earth is the center and the foundation upon which plant life and therefore animal life depend. Plants need animals to replenish the soil just as animals need plants to recycle the air. Modern America's food is deficient not in quantity but in the nutrients which define its quality. Soil shows depletion if plants are grown big in it but never thrown back in it, until eventually the plants show paltry growth and the animals that eat the plants show malnutrition.

Imagine a small suburban backyard garden supplying much of a family's vegetables for the summer and early fall. A vegetable gardener's predominant reason for cultivating his lot is concern with supplying his family with something nourishing. Yet, he'll use chemical fertilizers and chemical insecticides. A few do fertilize organically: rather than toss garbage into the trash, they compost kitchen and garden scraps in a corner of the yard. Some even go as far as to compost the weekly clippings from the lawns and the yearly leavings from the trees. A new generation is emerging whose symbol is the compost heap, not the garbage heap.

But one crucial link in nature's cycle is ignored by all: regenerating into the garden our very bodies. Instead, our families conceal our remains far away in some cemetery, as though garbage in some dump. Some of us even plot our escapes beforehand, prepaying for our sites, visiting them before our deaths, like little pharaohs devoting their lives to the construction of their pyramids. Usually these cemeteries, built outside of cities under the shadow of the smoking county incinerator, are relegated to the most desolate corners of society. Worse, our bodies are stuffed into airtight coffins into which the sands of time do not trickle for hundreds of years. And, worst of all, some of us are cremated: this could be best if ashes were returned to the wind or ground. But no, instead they are locked into urns. One English author's wife went so far as to mix her husband's ashes into a two-ton block of cement.

In contrast, George Bernard Shaw wished his ashes to be scattered in his garden, and suggested creating a law that a tree be planted for anyone who dies. Those whose bodies are buried in the simplest boxes of pine immediately inherit the earth by fertilizing lawns; but in a hundred years, when their names are forgotten by their sons and eroded off their tombstones, those lawns just might become farms or forests. Meanwhile, we dig our own graves, ignoring the cosmic fact that everything gotten must be given back.

Plants, animals, and humans are isogenous, and thus plants exist to nourish animals and humans, and they in turn exist to fertilize plants. The question "What is the purpose of human existence?" is sometimes answered "To raise children." If the purpose of our parents' lives were to give birth to us and ours is to give birth to their grandchildren, then the purpose of our parents' deaths is to nourish us and of ours to nourish their grandchildren. The answer really is: "To raise plants."

Thus, the problem of what to eat could be solved solely by knowing what food would cause our bodies to more adequately replenish the earth; both through the little parts of ourselves we leave behind every day and the lump sum we leave when we pass over to the other side of life. We, of course, could be eaten by carnivores, but carnivores also return to the soil, and so would we, though indirectly. Since the carnivore which eats other carnivores is the exception rather than the rule, this precludes our never returning to the soil by being fed to our children . . . unless we were vegetarians. But what vegetarians would raise their children as carnivores? What vegetarians would feed their children others' children?

We might nourish future generations more quickly and more directly by being buried at the trunk of a tree. We grow on fruits, fruits grow on trees, trees grow on us. One devoted son visits the apple tree which grows over his father's grave each fall, and gathers the apples which have fallen to the ground. For the following week he drinks and eats nothing but the juice from those apples, and does little else except write poetry. That poetry he dedicates to his father, hoping that completion will be reached through light which death would not permit through life.

Primitive humans probably survived larger predators since a carnivore's flesh is neither as sweet nor as soft as an herbivore's. The poet could not eat his father—that would have been very hard for him to have gotten down—but he can easily eat from the tree from which his father once ate and which now "eats" his father. He could also eat the squirrel that eats from the tree, but that places him twice removed from his father. Although the very closest he could get to his father would be to meet him in the world of the dead, as long as the poet remains in the world of the living he can get closest by eating the apples. Now it must be remembered that he is a poet and rarely speaks literally or historically, but usually metaphorically and allegorically, always tropologically, and in this case anagogically: the father is no father at all, but is the mother, Mother Earth.

Egoism, the opposite of Earth, is our deepest-rooted tendency which separates our individual goals from those which Mother Earth had intended. We act in the interest of Earth only when laboring under the delusion that these actions benefit only ourselves. Earth, understanding more than any individual, dupes us into serving her while we, who rarely understand ourselves and barely ever more than that, believe all along we are motivated by purely personal reasons. "Each false feeling produces the absolute certainty of having it," wrote Pier Paolo Pasolini. "My false feeling was that of health." (From the poem entitled, "A Desperate Vitality").

Our entire purpose in relation to plants is to fertilize them. Thus earth deludes us into believing we seek health for selfish effects when, in fact, it is for the sake of more consistent and more frequent bowel movements, that is, recyclable waste. And any who are embarrassed or simply bewildered by these scatological matters demonstrate their conditioning by a society which conceals the functions of the bathroom as much as of the slaughterhouse, a society which after all is on the side of Egoism, not of Earth.

Though Earth can dupe us, we can never dupe Earth; to try to do so is to dupe ourselves out of our health, or to dupe our grandchildren out of theirs, though health itself is a dupe. If we continue defecating into rivers rather than onto Earth—in the literal sense—the Earth will defecate on us—in the figurative sense. We can prepare ourselves to nourish our apple tree more directly, more immediately, by being nourished by it more directly: the laxative effect of fruit is well known. The fiber fad that swept the nation's intestines was not just nutritional but also ecological. In addition to adding bran to the diet, some people went further and reduced their consumption of flesh and white flour. Along with this, some even increased their intake of fresh fruits and fresh vegetables. Had they cut out flesh and white foods altogether, they could also have cut out the bran. The entire purpose of all their endeavors, which few could readily admit, was simply to develop better bowel movements.

What goes up must come down; what is born must die. Consider the apple and the squirrel side by side, the former fallen from a limb, the latter from a life. Granting fermentation in the apple and vermination in the squirrel, the apple on the ground disappears from sight by the first snow of winter, but the squirrel's body remains visible even after the last snow has melted under the spring sun. Just as fruit requires an hour for assimilation into the body, and flesh four or five, and just as fruit requires less time than flesh for decomposition into the earth, so maybe could a lean human body, nourished largely from fruit, decompose more quickly than a fatty one nourished from flesh. Karmically speaking, there must occur not only decomposition of the carnivore's body, but of all the consumed bodies within it.

Our whole role in this cycle is not merely a destiny to die, but to live until we die, and to excrete as much fertile waste as possible while we live. Merely eating a lot does not mean eating wisely, but produces only obesity, which, being a disease, induces improper digestion and unhealthy bowel movements: good bowel movements are a sign of good health, for what is good for Earth is good for ego. Thus Kafka's mother dog instructs her young puppies: "Water the ground as much as you can." (Anyone who reads Kafka's "Investigations of a Dog" after having read Dostoyevsky's *Notes from the Underground*, and "The Burrow" after Defoe's *Robinson Crusoe*, will understand the reason for Kafka's vegetarianism.) This duty to Earth explains dogs' instinct to water at the trunks of trees, to return to Earth what they have taken from her as directly and as immediately as possible, particularly because of their carnivorism. "Instinct" is used here to explain what humans cannot explain in animals, what humans have long ago forgotten and shall probably never know again.

Since most of us are city-dwellers, we have forgotten everything we were born with and, like our predecessors the cave-dwellers, have naturally adapted to our environment, though the environment itself is unnatural. If we are the highest form of animal life, and if we are to eat plants, these might as well be mostly the highest form of plants, trees, that is, fruits and nuts from trees. But Coke and pizza, and Big Mac and small potatoes are our fare. Such is the consequence of eating what is local to the environment. Fire hydrants memorialize where trees once grew, and our dogs too have adapted to our environment.

All final conclusions can be reached by deduction and if truly final can be verified by observation. City streets illustrate differences between two diets by what two fellow mammals leave behind: dog feces and horse feces. The former forces perturbed pedestrians to abandon all intended paths, while the latter hardly attracts the nose's attention, and even when fresh, has an earthy quality. Horses eat oats; dogs eat horses.

Ego echoes Earth just as digestion echoes decomposition and fertilization. Consider, furthermore, the protein combination needed to supply the human body with balanced amino acids when their sources are non-animal and partially cooked: one-part legume to three-parts grain, nut or seed; or expressed another way, one-part legume to one-part grain to one-part nut to one-part seed. Now consider the crop rotation necessary to prevent farmland depletion: one year of legumes alternated with two or three years of grains or other vegetables. Hence combination echoes rotation.

Has enough been said, or too much? Just as air in a sealed space without plants becomes poisonous to animals, thought without reflection becomes ridiculous. We should take a breather to contemplate whether what has been said through a series of sorites, began in the sublime only to pass away as a sortie into absurdity, or whether at the crossroads the right way was chosen and, though detoured from the straight path of epistemology, we somehow ended a little closer to the truth than where we began. It is not for nothing that the ancients sought oracles by sorting through the feces of animals.

*   *   *

Even if in apparent opposition like acid and alkaline, sodium and potassium, or yin and yang, two diets might combine well together, throw light on one another, and complement each other as do soy and oats on the breakfast table, or red and green on the color wheel. A lazy mind would grasp only where they differ, an active mind also where they agree. To better evaluate vegetarianism we would do well to contemplate carnivorism. But why look up close at what stinks of blood and gore from a distance? Like attracts like, but that which reeks repels everything—except maggots. Those who smoke tobacco have every right to stay stuck in their own muck. Just as smokers are separated from non-smokers in trains and planes, someday so will be carnivores from non-carnivores in restaurants and dining halls. To those with a nose as clear as their conscience, burning flesh is far more nauseating a smell than burning tobacco.

The question "What's for supper?" has a long history. Answers have been as diverse as Western philosophies, world religions, social dogmas, and political platforms. Yet no one *must* reason or believe or conform or vote; but everyone must eat. "So what's for supper, Mom?" In the Arctic, the answer is fish or part of a walrus; in Tahiti, mango or part of a coconut. Climates differ, available food differs, and what in fact differs most is what is suitable to each environment. The body temperature of a walrus is warmer than the Artic snow, so the Eskimos eat walrus to keep themselves warm; but the center of a fruit is cooler than its skin exposed to the tropic sun, so Polynesians eat fruit to keep themselves cool. Climate also directly affects racial origin which in turn affects dietary needs. In America, home of the mongrel, where Mom's answer often is the hot dog, a Chinese American living in Chinatown thrives on a diet different from an Italian American's in Little Italy, though they share the same block in downtown Manhattan.

When introduced to someone for the first time, we are so impatient. We foolishly believe that someone can be summarized in a sentence. So we ask the person's astrological sign, or numerological designation, or sexual orientation, or age, or occupation, or favorite music, or favorite food . . . or forbidden food. Also we ask ethnic origin. Mainland and menu are the same; people spring from their foods which spring from their soils. In the end, we are asking from what earth the person had come, and wondering into what earth the body shall go.

The choice is between eating ignorantly what a society, carnivorous and hospitalized, says we should, or wisely what Earth wants of us.

The ritual of eating wisely, however, could itself become an obsession and a waste of time, indeed the three-point pivot around which might revolve the whole of the day. Those who observe the strictest food-combining laws sometimes simplify the number of daily meals to two: one of fruit, the other of vegetables. These people enjoy their food as much as anyone else; they just do not devote the whole of the day to indulging in it.

After persistently and consciously guiding the hands to feed the mouth the right food, the mind can trust its hands to reach correctly out of habit. But until such a stage is reached we might wonder, as a young carnivorous king did, just what single book on vegetarian nutrition to read. The young king had several wise men and women at his disposal and knew not what to do with them. So he sent them off, instructing them to write a single treatise on the theory and practice of vegetarian nutrition for transitional carnivores. The result was a book which did not demand much and did not tell the whole truth, but only the germ. But the king was clearly told what to do and how to do it; as many formulas as recipes accompanied the text. The name of the book was *Diet for a Small Planet*, and the wise men assumed the collective pseudonym of Frances M. Lappé.

It had taken ten years to write; none of the wise men had retired or died, so the middle-aged king sent them out again. This time he instructed them to simplify the menu, to exclude sea animals entirely, and to de-emphasize protein in general and milk and eggs in particular. The king had become somewhat wise himself and could point the way. For another ten years the men pondered and labored, then called their second book *Nutrition Survival Kit*. Its two-fold format alternated between theory and practice from chapter to chapter. Too obviously the work of many minds, the wise men collectively used two names, Kathy Dinaburg and D'Ann Akel.

The king's health remained quite wonderful, but since he could afford it he sought more. He sent the old men away again, this time for forty years in the desert, where they prepared a book partially about feeding the body and partially about nourishing the soul. They had understood that total health came from not merely proper food, but from exercise, sunlight, air and rest. Realizing that all parts of the human being—not just the body—needed cultivation, along with their raw food vegetarian diet they fasted regularly and practiced yoga and meditation. Many were planning to live into the next millennium, and their book told how they intended to do it. Its title was *Survival into the 21st Century*. They all wore long beards and longer hair, and conjured up an exceedingly strange name for themselves: Viktoras Kulvinskas. Some now walked with canes, and two had died—at the ages of 131 and 135. But by this time the king had abandoned his diet and showed greater age than the older wise men.

Royalty leads a hard life, the king said, and has demanding schedules; also he said he could not offend the aristocrats and diplomats of other nations by refusing to dine at their tables. This was a silly worry, for the king could hardly talk, walk, or feed himself. In fact, the new book was useless to him because he could no longer see to read it. So he instructed the remaining ten men to revisit the desert and to return only after condensing all vegetarian nutritional knowledge into one sentence.

For forty days and forty nights the wise men fasted. They devised their final edict after much deliberation, and after equal deliberation all but one decided the desert was where they wished to make their home. So the solitary wise man returned and whispered into the old king's ear: "We grow on fruits, fruits grow on trees, trees grow on us: everything gotten must be given back."

He then broke his fast on grapes, and while he ate, the king looked on. The king made some feeble motions signifying that he had not understood what was spoken, for the king was now nearly deaf, dumb, and blind. So the wise man knelt down and placed in the king's sweaty hand a single grape. The king held it in his palm like the half-blind father embracing his prodigal son. He then understood everything, inhaled one last smell of the sweet air, and passed over into the other side of life. The wise man buried him in a vineyard, where the only marker was the grapevine he now nourished.

*   *   *

Nutrition is not an ever-expanding realm of research in which seekers must keep informed of recent developments: the latest weight-loss fad, the newest miracle vitamin discovery, the most innovative aging preventative invention. Rather, it diminishes to simpler and simpler irrefutable laws. The entire question of what to eat could be condensed to the answer of a single grape, which is complexity itself.

The history of human society appears to be unraveling backwards: that is, from the simple to the complex. Our modern economies revolve around our inability to do things for ourselves, and thus our dependence on others. Humans are strange creatures who eat animals but rarely eat what they kill. A mouse heard one night within the wall of a house will find traps set in the morning; but few humans kill in the morning the cow they intend to eat for supper. Neither killing nor eating animals is to be condoned, but the one vice seems to de-vice the other when done together. The sight, sound, smell, and certainty of death attracts even the cowardly, particularly if the death of an enemy or a criminal. Men more willingly risk their lives at war when chances appear certain for the enemy's defeat. In the same vein, public hangings were once as great a social event as our summer Sunday church chicken barbecues. The basic attraction for flesh foods is, of course, contained in the taste of blood, but also in the security of its being someone else's. If nations " . . . shall beat their swords into plowshares, and their spears into pruning hooks" (Isaiah 2:4), all swords, not just war swords, must be transformed; rather than possess both butcher knives and plowshares, we must keep only the one. Yet we concern ourselves not with plowshares, swords, or knives, but with shopping carts. Unlike primitive hunters who risked their lives killing animals, Diana housewives of the supermarket hunt risk theirs eating them.

Nature's laws, which abhor superfluities as much as vacuums, command simplicity, and this means the simplest diet. But just as two things similar are not the same, no two people find the same things simple. Thus vegetarianism varies from mere omission of flesh to near fruitarianism. Whatever way is followed, so long as it is accompanied by vitamin pills, the way is not simple enough; any need for pills is an acknowledgement of the inadequacy of the diet. They are a medicine to be taken for as long as disease persists, but no longer than needed and as little as possible. Mega-doses are contradictory to their whole aim: no great talent or thought is necessary to take as much as possible, the only limiting factor being the purse. However, if a vitamin is used as medicine, the supplicant need not falsify the highest standards nor pander to the lowest. Vitamins are needed to assimilate the protein and minerals in food—a task difficult to accomplish by the body that suffers from malnourishment due in part to lack of vitamins. Pills can actually be crucial for a smooth transition from plastic foods to plant foods, from the nugatory to the natural.

Ours is an age of convenience typified by pills and potions, and an age of impatience betrayed by automobiles which rush to red lights and speed to stop signs. Not thankful for having a banana from thousands of miles away, most mix ingratitude with impatience by rarely eating it at its fully-ripened black or brown. Or, realizing that a yellow or green banana is unripe, but unwilling to wait for a week, some bake or fry it. A pot of whole wheat berries simmered for three hours is more digestible than one quickly boiled for half an hour, and more nourishing than white instant farina to which boiling water is added in the breakfast bowl. Imagine the greater value of a seven-day shoot of wheat grass! Patience being the first criterion for indoor sprouting, eventually patience grows with the sprouts, and we can pass our days sitting on the front porch watching the grass grow.

Patience also is necessary for dietary transitions. The slower the transition, the more stable the result. As in love, impatience forms only loose bonds to the ideal to which we are committed. Typical beginnings lead to typical ends, or to total catastrophe.

This happened to the old man who had spent all his life searching for the fountain of youth. One day he found it and, forgetting everything—his age, his arthritis, and his obesity—he jumped right in and drowned. But even through error we gain some access to a higher ideal; so long as we are ahead of the world, we can afford to go slowly. In chewing food, the one who chews the most slowly wins. Likewise in choosing foods.

A life contains not time enough to know everything about ourselves or even everything about nutrition, but a few months is enough to know for ourselves all we need to know about nutrition. The months, however, should not be consecutive, but separated by years. Ten years to assure a smooth transition from cooked carnivorism to raw vegetarianism is not long compared to the thousands taken the other way around. Eleven basic steps might be outlined, one for each year, not all of which need be done, nor one by one.

The foothold from which our whole discussion springs is exemplified by sirloin steak, supplemented by dad's backyard barbecued hot dogs and mom's homemade apple pies. Less loved children learn to settle for Big Mac and Pop Tarts. The book addressed directly to this vast populace is the best seller *Diet for a Small Planet*. Its substitution of fish for flesh, of milk for meat, is comparable to switching from white sugar to raw sugar, from a high-tar cigarette to a low. A second step is lacking here; cutting out merely mammal meat and poultry is not enough. The other two staples of the American diet, white flour and white sugar, also must go. Otherwise, such vegetarianism, whose adherents are hardly healthier than before, is the type which has most to gain from a little peek into almost any additional sources.

Two excellent Step Two books, both by Paavo Airola, worthy of investigation at this point are *How To Get Well* and *Are You Confused?* Here we find out what is so unhealthful about all those white foods, why we need to eat produce fresh, how little protein we really need, and so on. Fish and sea animals are still eaten, however . . . until one day, while gobbling lobster, the story is heard of how the animal was mercilessly thrown into boiling water and allowed to struggle in torment until sinking into oblivion, now the soup of suffering in our spoons.

Thus at Step Three the animals of the sea join the ranks of those of the land, and all are left better safe than quarry. Now that neither sickness nor confusion is the primary concern, good reading material would be Kathy Dinaburg and D'Ann Akel's *Nutrition Survival Kit*. About neither backpacking in forests nor retreating to fallout shelters, it advises how to survive in an equally treacherous environment, the modern kitchen.

Until this point we have been lacto-ovo-vegetarians, but soon we realize that dairy in the diet causes as much mucus to flow from the nose as blood from the calf's neck: at Step Four we wean away from Mother Cow. Step Five, when we stay away from what the chickens lay away, occurs as often before Step Four as after, and more usually right along with it. Although many macrobiotics eat sea animals, Steps Four and Five conform to macrobiotic principles; so here many of George Ohsawa's works are valuable, particularly the introductory *Macrobiotics: An Invitation to Health and Happiness*.

Essentially a gourmet's guide to nutrition as well as to philosophy, macrobiotics has its limitations. Its followers may easily tire of the waste of valuable time devoted to chopping and frying and boiling and baking. Objections could also arise to its many omissions and contradictions: overemphasis on cooked grains and beans to the exclusion of fresh fruits, seasalting everything despite the plentiful inclusion of sea vegetables, fresh vegetables of the earth cooked to the consistency of those from cans, and the devotion of a large part of the literature to the cure of ailments which no one is supposed to contract.

So Step Six slowly supersedes Five: fresh fruits become a main staple, vegetables are eaten only raw, salt is excluded altogether, and the few ailments about which we might complain are quickly cured simply by fasting. All this is basically the regimen of Paul Bragg's writings, of which the key book is *The Miracle of Fasting*.

With Step Seven the health food store and produce market totally supersede the supermarket, where we now go only for bathroom and kitchen supplies. The kitchen itself becomes limited in use and larger in space, with the discarding of the stove and oven. We learn to turn off the gas, which was a sort of laughing gas, for the laugh was on us. We might even imitate Johnny Appleseed and wear pots on our heads: that would be our only remaining use for them. By this time, at least ninety-five percent of our food is raw, that is, no more than one cooked meal a week. This step puts us on the path of the Natural Hygiene movement, whose one best book among many is Herbert Shelton's *Health for the Millions*. We learn not only what to eat, but when to eat, what to eat together, and when not to eat altogether. Fresh fruits eaten with seeds or nuts are good, but eaten alone are better; fresh vegetables eaten alone are good, but eaten with nuts or seeds are better; fruits and vegetables are never to be eaten together; and best of all are those days when we eat nothing at all.

A kind of fruitarianism evolves at Step Eight. Actually this includes nuts and seeds from the health food store, and sprouts and grasses from our own windowsill gardens. Fruitarianism in its broadest sense does not entail eating only fruits, but rather the selected substitution of foods which fall from the plant for those which are the plants themselves. Thus apples and berries are "fruit-fruits"; almonds and Brazils are "nut-fruits"; sesame and sunflower are "seed-fruits"; and peppers and pumpkins are "vegetable-fruits." While the tomato is a "fruit," the potato is not. And sprouts, not quite a vegetable but only a short time ago a seed or a bean or a nut, are the best of both worlds. There is no one perfect food, but just as the egg is the most nearly perfect for the carnivore, the fruit and the sprout are for the vegetarian.

Yet we are not talking about perfection, nor even about how to reach perfection; all we are discussing is how to reach. The single crucial volume for this step is Viktoras Kulvinskas' *Survival into the 21st Century*. If we had to be our own wise men and read but one book on vegetarian nutrition, this would be the one.

The healthier vegetarians are those of us whose diets rest somewhere along Steps Six, Seven, and Eight; these are the steps about which more detailed discourse can be found elsewhere in this book (chapters 3 and 8).

And then, Step Nine, "fruit-fruitarianism." Many fanatic, scientific vegetarians denigrate this even more than carnivorism, but why can't we dream? After all, people dreamed for thousands of years about landing on the moon before actually accomplishing the feat. Given the right raw material, a pure body should be able to manufacture everything it needs, protein and B12 included. Fruit is that right raw material, but no one is sure what a pure body is or if it is any more possible today to have a pure body than to have pure air. Arnold Ehret's *Mucusless Diet Healing System*, the seminal treatise on "fruit-fruitarianism," instructs that one way to maintain a pure body is through fasting. (Ehret himself might have been the model for Kafka's "Hunger Artist.") Of course, no one need strive to get here, or to stop here. There are even times when we may need to retreat to old treats, the way a car stuck in the mud must first drive in reverse before further attempting to go forward. So long as we progress slowly enough to know where our particular bodies work best, to know where to turn back if everything doesn't feel fine and to know our bodily functions well enough to recognize when something is wrong, then, like Zeno's approach to the wall which is never reached but gets ever closer, we might limit even the variety of fruit. No one reaches any stage of finality in life except by dying.

If all goes well, Step Ten awaits, the number of completion and perfection according to Pythagorean numerology. We might eat only two meals a day and only two different daily fruits, one for each meal. Consider the apple and the banana—the least expensive and most available. Next we might choose between the apple and the banana, and if we live in a non-tropical zone, the apple might suffice. Unlike the banana, it flourishes in our own northerly climates and possesses no wasteful skin to throw away. Its dozen seeds provide protein, its one or two leaves nearest the stem some chlorophyll. The apple might represent Step Eleven, the itemizer of the ideal, and humanity's first food from the Fall could become its last before the return of Paradise.

It is no coincidence that the chief cause of death in the domasticated [sic] animal world is slaughter, while in the human world it is starvation. While one half of the human world diets, the other half dies. As terrible as all the animal lives wasted are all the human lives lost or led astray. The goal is not just to reduce desire for any particular food, or for all foods, but to reduce all desires. The person obsessed by ten desires who satisfies five of them is only half as happy as the person who has one desire and satisfies it.

So what if we desire only apples? That is still a desire which must be satisfied. So we could aim straight for Step Twenty-Two, the number of expansion and ascension, the Master Number, though only in a material sense, and we might transcend food altogether. Dust collects over everything we eat, until eventually it is all we eat. Ultimately we would reach down into the ground, pull up a handful of earth, and eat it: to eat what we would become. Another way of saying that someone died is: "He bit the dust."

"How much land does a man need?" asked Tolstoy in a short story by that name. The answer: "About six feet by two."

3. Letter to a Young Vegetarian: A Postprandial Pasticcio

Socrates: So the man in training ought to regulate his actions and exercises and eating and drinking by the judgment of his instructor, who has expert knowledge, rather than by the opinions of the rest of the public . . . Now if he disobeys the one man and disregards his opinion and commendations, and pays attention to the advice of many who have no expert knowledge, surely he will suffer some bad effect . . . And what is this bad effect? Where is it produced? I mean, in what part of the disobedient person?

Crito: His body, obviously; that is what suffers . . .

Socrates: Then consider the next step. There is a part of us which is improved by healthy actions and ruined by unhealthy ones. If we spoil it by taking the advice of nonexperts, will life be worth living when this part is once ruined? The part I mean is the body . . . Well, is life worth living with a body which is worn out and ruined in health?

Crito: Certainly not.

PLATO
Crito, 47

What we are going to engage in now is strictly straight talk, as two good friends from far away and long ago do in an exchange of letters. The following letter is quite real, and the reply equally real; but for the sake of argument let us say they are imaginary. On the one hand, we could outline some nutritional advice to apply to everyone, though forsaking our own rather narrow views; on the other hand, we could forget everyone entirely and just speak of what is right for ourselves alone. Let us endeavor to draw our line somewhere near the median of the two menus, with no claim to finality and, we hope, no suggestion of arbitrariness. And let us remember that anything written here can as well be found elsewhere in a hundred other books and a thousand magazines and ten thousand newspapers in the past ten years.

Dear Mark,

I am interested in a raw food diet without the use of eggs, milk, dairy, fish, fowl or meat. Also, I don't want to eat any food that needs to be blenderized or extensively refrigerated. (I intend to only temporarily use a refrigerator for greens until I can grow plants in a greenhouse or in pots.)

I am looking for specific advice—I've read books that say only, for example, that one can get calcium from sesame seeds, but neglect to say exactly how much to eat for my age, height, and weight.

I am 22 years old, 166 cm. and weigh 55 kg.

My questions are:

1) *How do I get enough protein? How much of which foods?*
2) *Calcium—How much of which foods per day?*
3) *Iron—How much of which foods per day?*
4) *Iodine—How much of which foods per day? (I don't want to use salt.)*
5) *B12—Is nutritional yeast really healthful or necessary? Other foods?*
6) *Is there an alternative to wheat germ? That is, another food with the same amount of minerals and vitamins? My main argument against wheat germ is that it needs refrigeration.*
7) *Any other advice about a raw food diet would be appreciated.*
8) *Are supplements necessary?*

I hope you can advise me. Also, will you list any qualifications you might have?

Peace and peas
MARGIE

Dear Margie,

No one can give you specific advice. You tell your physical characteristics, but what about your nationality and mentality, climate and housemate, altitude and attitude, disposition and occupation, recreation and aspiration? As great a difference exists between the minds of a genius and a fool as between a monkey and a mollusk. Likewise between their bodies. Hippocrates called the human being "That infinitely variable organism without which human disease is impossible." Everyone of different cultural and chromosomal heritage has different nutritional needs.

Furthermore, two identical twins leading different lives, and if male, marrying different wives, consequently eat, and need to eat, different foods.

An office worker under a fluorescent lamp needs more vitamin A, an urbanite among automobile exhaust pipes more C, a northerner always in the shade more D, someone under stress extra Bs, etc. The science of nutrition speaks for all humans and completely forsakes the individual. For this reason, MDRs and RDAs should be discarded in the garbage heap along with the AMA and the FDA. No book can give the specific information you seek. Only you know when you are hungry, and only you know when you are full. Only you know what foods you like—which, if your body is relatively pure, is also what is good for you—and only you know what foods you dislike—which, hopefully, your body is reading correctly. The question might be how to assure a pure body. The fast way is to fast. The slow and sure way is the raw, or mostly raw, vegetarian diet.

The eater is one variable, the eaten another. Sunlight, soil, water, and seed all vary; so, therefore, do vitamin and mineral contents. Storage further alters everything: an orange eaten right off the tree in Florida has more than twice the vitamin C as another orange off the same branch eaten two months later in Canada. Let us say only that more C is found in an orange than an apple, so if you seek a lot of C eat more oranges than apples. We have not said how much C is in an orange, how much C you need, or how many oranges you need to eat. Be suspicious of any table or chart which tells how much C *you* need or how much more C is in an orange than an apple. The most we should say is "Eat apples and oranges."

Weigh the first set of variables concerning who is eating on one pan, and the second set concerning what is eaten on the other. If you can balance the scales and read the measurement, your vision is sharper than mine. Faith in absolute uniformity can lead to pill popping: a person reads on a label that so-and-so pill supplies 500 mgs of C, reads in a book that so-and-so person needs 1000 mgs, and puts 500 and 500 together to get . . . a person who pops two pills a day for the prevention of colds, who increases to four at the first sign of a cold, who increases to ten a day during a cold, and who somehow fails to question the cause of the cold.

You've given the example of calcium from sesame seeds. Calciums don't count. I would no sooner count each milligram of calcium than each seed of sesame.

1. How do I get enough protein? How much of which foods?

Twenty years ago some sources said we needed one hundred grams of protein per day; ten years ago, eighty grams; now sixty, or one gram daily for every kilogram of body weight. If the count-down continues, in another twenty years they'll be telling us twenty grams. If you eat raw, and if you count, perhaps all you need is twenty; but this measurement depends on who you are. And when eating raw, you needn't worry about complementarity because complete protein is found in green leafy vegetables and sprouts, and because the incomplete protein of nuts and seeds will most likely be eaten with complete ones. Keep in mind the food-combining laws, and eat nuts and seeds with vegetables. Better still, sprout seeds, grains, and beans *into* vegetables. It is hardly mere chance that general laws for food combining enforce those specifically for protein combining.

While no salad can be considered a reliable quantitative source of protein when served meagerly as a side dish to steak and pota-toes, enough can be found when the whole meal is a large bowl of greens. Unsprouted seeds and nuts are nearly complete, particu-larly sesame and almonds; you might get along if all you ate were either of these. But we are not talking about eating one protein food only. Incidentally, mixed nuts with peanuts (which are peas, not nuts) are cheaper but more complete in protein than mixtures without. But eat them raw and unsalted: roasting and frying destroy the high-quality nut oils, while the cooking oils are usually of the lowest grade. Salt inhibits the digestion of any-thing eaten with it, and particularly of oils.

Some find raw and unsalted nuts already difficult to digest. All nuts taste better, are chewed more easily, and are digested more efficiently if soaked for a day. Or soak them for half a day, and sprout them a day or two more. If they are eaten dry, chew each at least thirty-two times, once for each tooth. You can grind nuts and seeds in a blender one cup at a time and add water to make a paste. If you add the soak water from a previous batch that sat in a warm place for a day, and set aside that mixture for another day, you will have fermented the paste into cheese if the batch is thick or into yogurt if it is thin. My favorite is almond, then sun-flower. Add kelp and other herb seasonings to what you plan to eat with vegetables, and add fennel, anise, or caraway to those to be eaten with fruits.

Nut milks are excellent quick preparations. First, grind the dry nuts in the blender, then add a much larger proportion of fruit juice, then perhaps a banana. My favorite milk is cashew. Of course, an objection to blenderizing is well founded because the heat generated by the blade mildly "cooks" whatever it is blending or grinding. But seeds such as sesame, chia, flax and psyllium usually pass through the system whole, no matter how much they are chewed, unless they are ground. Those three latter seeds gel into thick shakes when mixed with juice, and into delicious puddings when mixed with whipped fruits such as soaked apricots, dates or figs.

No discussion of protein is complete without mention of brewer's or nutritional yeast. Yeast is ever so slightly deficient in the essential amino acid methionine, so eat one or two Brazil nuts with it. In fact, many otherwise complete protein foods are ever so slightly deficient in methionine; just keep in mind that Brazil nuts are the highest source.

2. Calcium—How much of which foods per day?

You've already spoken of sesame seed. You may or may not believe the controversy over oxalic acid in their hulls: some say it combines with calcium into an indigestible compound. I eat those with hulls because that is the way they come naturally, and being natural, they stay fresher far longer. Besides, dehulling processes are either chemical—in which case a residue remains which burns a hole in your stomach—or mechanical—in which case the cost is prohibitive, and burns a hole in your pocketbook. I have no trouble with oxalic acid; as is true with spinach, the trouble probably occurs when the seed and its hull are heated.

In the raw diet, the foods high in protein are also high in calcium: seeds, nuts, and green leaves. The darker the green, the better. Thus the typical American cuisine rests its plastic, gassed tomatoes atop a leafy bed of green so light as to appear almost white, iceberg lettuce. And did you know that as much calcium may be found in a glass of carrot juice as in an equal amount of cow's milk? The fresh carrot juice is not pasteurized, as is most milk, so in terms of calcium the carrot is preferable to the cow.

3. Iron—How much of which foods per day?

Iron-rich foods are the same foods you should eat for protein and for calcium. You should see a pattern emerging. Pumpkin seeds are an incredibly rich source of iron, and plenty is found in fruits, particularly the variety that dry readily, whether eaten dry or fresh. Drying is the least detrimental of all preservative processes, but it is still important to restore all dried fruits to their original consistency by soaking. Digestion is improved; and since dried fruit sticks to the teeth with greater tenacity than honey, the one source of cavities in a raw food diet will be eliminated by soaking. Honey-dipped fruit—the honey is used as a preservative—eaten dry is worst of all.

If you have to settle for sulphured fruits, throw out the soak water after half an hour and cover the fruit in water again. Under all other circumstances, drink the soak water; it's juice. About juices: drink only those freshly squeezed if you wish to drink them at all, though your teeth are more efficient juicers than any machine. Juices in bottles and cartons are all pasteurized. Frozen concentrates are condensed in ways other than evaporation, so they are a smaller form of the same old non-food. Health food stores carry unpasteurized whole frozen juices, and a brand of bottled juice heated well below standard pasteurizing temperatures. This latter juice tastes almost as good as fresh; as though indeed fresh, it frequently turns bad on the store shelves. But the difference is this: something fresh ferments, while once cooked it turns rotten. Food must first be good before it can become bad; those which rarely turn bad were probably never good. Sometimes the next best thing to, or improvement upon, water fasting is fruit juice fasting, which is not really fasting at all but feasting. This brings us back to the subject of iron. A friend once entered the hospital for a week because of broken bones from an auto accident. Her diet was vegetarian but basically macrobiotic: that is, everything cooked. Upon arrival, blood analysis revealed her red blood cell count to be low. In the hospital she ate only the fresh fruits provided by the hospital, which were their only wholesome foods, and fresh fruit and vegetable juices supplied by me. Upon departure, her count was "normal."

4. *Iodine—How much of which foods per day?*
   (I don't want to use salt.)

An inorganic mineral no more fit for human consumption than a handful of soil, salt found its way into our diet from its use as a preservative of flesh. Everyone needs sodium and iodine, but no one needs salt. You get lots of sodium in earth vegetables, partic-

ularly carrots, celery and beets, and plenty of iodine in sea vegetables. You need not cook them though they come dry: hiziki
and arame are ready to eat after soaking half a day, and wakame
after a day or two. Cover them three times over in water, and
drink that water. Dulse need not be soaked at all; it tastes like
potato chips. When speaking of sea vegetables, we are not talking
merely about iodine, but about every trace mineral from the sea.
Sea salt has them too, but is still mostly sodium chloride. The
difference between sea salt and earth salt is like that between
raw sugar and white sugar—and that is not much of a difference.
Use kelp in place of salt; though heat-dried, its benefits outweigh
its single pinch of unworthiness. Buy it by the pound, not the
shaker. Mix one-part kelp to one-part parsley, basil, crushed
sesame, etc. This herbal mixture goes wonderfully with
avocados or vegetable salads.

5. *B12—Is nutritional yeast really healthful or
necessary? Other foods?*

The question most often asked of complete vegetarians is
"Where do you get your protein?" The next most frequent question is "What about vitamin B12?" The whole nutritional argument for complete vegetarianism either stands or falls on this
issue.

**Officials warn that abstinence from
flesh, milk, and eggs is as sure a cause of
pernicious anemia as indulgence in tobacco is of cancer; yet mothers will react
with greater horror on learning that their
children have stopped drinking milk and
eating eggs than that they had started
smoking cigarettes.**

In fact, the vegetarian who would develop anemia eats very poorly and probably smokes cigarettes. George Bernard Shaw suffered
from anemia late in his life, but if we judge from the sweet garbage in the recipe book written by his cook, he deserved his disease. White foods and cooked carbohydrates will lead to disabil-
ity for anyone, and especially someone past the age when most
people have died.

It is probable that millennia before our forebears ate flesh they produced B12 in their bodies, the way most herbivores do today. Our bodies had to be pure to encourage intestinal growth of beneficial bacteria, the same strain now responsible for production of the vitamin in mold cultures for manufacture into pills. When humans began eating flesh and cooking it, and cooking everything else they ate with it, putrefaction occurred in the intestines and the beneficial bacteria no longer found an environment suitable for growth. Although cooking considerably limits the usable amounts, enough surplus B12 was assimilated.

From survival to revival, the raw vegetarian diet rises above the futility of flesh eating like a phoenix out of the fire. Once your body is cleansed through periodic fasting and continues to be kept relatively pure through proper diet—in which case you need not fast, or not so often—the intestines should again become the home of friendly bacteria.

Yet the problem is not just of production, but of absorption. Even carnivores taking pills with potencies of 1,000 mcgs can remain deficient. The cure then is direct injection of the vitamin into the bloodstream. This could be the key which opens the door for raw foods for all, though no one is forced to enter: B12 is found in or on plants, but in amounts so small that cooking destroys all of it, and a toxic body assimilates none of it. The elusive nutrient is found in sea vegetables and algae, and in fermented foods such as miso and nut cheeses. It is also produced by micro-organisms found on fruits and vegetables as long as no pesticides or fungicides inhibit their growth. This means sticking as strictly as possible to organically grown foods. Such foods also do not need rinsing, which is an added benefit, since all B vitamins are water soluble. Speaking of rinsing, the micro-organism is found in most batches of sprouts.

All this information was gathered from vegetarian periodicals and books written by zealots occasionally as full of baloney and guilty of fabrications and misrepresentations as those by any other fanatic intent on changing the world. So don't believe any of the above facts; just consider the following figures: I have been a complete vegetarian since 1970, and am alive and quite well, thank you. And how are you? Still unconvinced? Worry will harm you more than any vitamin deficiency, so go ahead and take a 50 mcg pill once a week. They are completely vegetarian, and of natural origin. Or eat a tablespoon a day of nutritional yeast, but the kind with the B12 added.

This brings on the next question.

6. *Is there an alternative to wheat germ? That is, another
food with the same amount of minerals and vitamins? My
main argument against wheat germ is that it needs
refrigeration.*

Wheat germ is a fractured food, essentially no more wholesome than the white flour from which it came. It has all those
vitamins, minerals, and protein which the white flour does not
have, but unlisted on its label is its rancidity, also uncharacteris-
tic of the white flour. As important as eating foods raw is eating
foods whole. Wheat kernels will keep fresh for years, raw wheat
germ for but a few days. As you say, it needs refrigeration, or better still, freezing. Raw wheat germ when fresh is golden yellow
and tastes sweet, but most of those brands found on store shelves
are dull brown and taste terrible. Toasted wheat germ does not
deteriorate as quickly, but that is because much of its value is initially destroyed in the toasting process. The alternative to wheat
germ is simply the whole wheat kernel either sprouted or grown
into grass.

Once nature's protective coatings are penetrated, foods must
be wrapped in the very large and cumbersome shell, the refrigerator. If you are unwilling to purchase a refrigerator, then buy
your nuts unshelled, your seeds unhulled. Unrefined, expeller-
pressed oils are also fractured foods, and so must be chilled—but
they are unnecessary in a diet that includes lots of nuts and
seeds. One food with as much nutritional benefit as wheat germ
and which needs no refrigeration is brewer's yeast. But it tastes
far more terrible than rancid wheat germ. Anything with such a
taste must be of sinister derivation, and indeed it is: alcohol.
Primary-grown yeasts, also called nutritional yeasts, which taste
somewhat better, also are of a doubtful origin: molasses.

Yet there is neither alcohol in brewer's yeast, nor molasses in
those primary-grown. Although they are heat-dried, they are
excellent additions to a morning's glass of orange juice. Half a
banana in the blender overwhelms the yeast taste wonderfully.
Baker's yeast, used to raise bread, is live so it fits right in the raw
food diet; it also tastes better. But it must be eaten only in the
morning with nothing other than water to wash it down; otherwise, it will ferment the food mixed with it and cause flatulence.
Flatulence may also result from too much brewer's yeast when
eaten by an enthusiastic beginner; but its bad taste acts as a safe-
ty valve. The best juices to mix with yeast are grapefruit, grape,
orange, and apple, particularly apple cider, which happens to be

the one fresh juice commonly sold in markets. Start small, a half a teaspoon daily for a week, a teaspoon for a month, and increase slowly to no more than four tablespoons: you do not need more than that amount of protein in one meal.

Another high-protein, vitamin- and mineral-rich food is bee pollen. The pollen is actually the flower's, the labor in gathering it the bee's. Like honey, it is an animal product which finds its way onto our plates only by exploitation of the insect's labors. A trapdoor device at the entrance to the hive brushes off the pellets of pollen the bees gathered for the hive—not for humans—and the wings and legs often found in an unsifted haul attest to the cruelty of stealing it from its rightful owners. Is it not bad enough that we rob them of honey and force them to feed on sugar water? Worse still is our making off with their pollen and royal jelly. Even if you do not object to killing insects, even those which are not our competitors, why need anyone harass and insult the one little creature, besides the earthworm, that is the plant world's most beneficial ally? Besides, the cost of bee pollen is outrageously high, almost an arm and a leg.

All things considered—the rancidity of wheat germ, the flatulency of brewer's yeast, the expediency of bee pollen—the answer to your question about nutritious food is: eat anything listed in William Esser's *Dictionary of Man's Foods*, a compendium of descriptions of fruits, vegetables, nuts and seeds.

7. *Any other necessary advice about a raw food diet would be appreciated.*

Eat it raw, or not at all. Nutrition tells us what is good, but cookery produces what merely tastes good. Likewise, exercise produces health but cosmetics only the illusion of health. This leads to your next question, for in the modern American bathroom cabinet, along with the medicine and the cosmetics, are also found the vitamin pills.

8. *Are supplements necessary?*

Do not be fooled: no such thing exists as a natural vitamin pill. Even those labeled natural are mostly synthetic. No Bs greater than 10 mgs come from food sources, nor Cs greater than 100 mgs. The Bs are usually chemicals added to a base of brewer's yeast; the Cs to a base of rose hips or acerola. Even when the pill is of a natural origin, such as A, D, and E, beginning has little to do with end, since various chemical processes are employed in extraction, separation, and preservation. The A and D come from fish liver oils, anyway, and are encapsulated in animal gelatin.

The concept of a natural pill is self-contradictory. In what grove does the vitamin C tablet grow? In what field the E capsule stalk? Vitamine E oil is extracted from wheat germ oil via wheat germ via wheat: is that natural? While the eater of sprouted wheat needs no extra E, the typical form of edible wheat is flour, whose milling process oxidizes the E, and then as bread, whose baking burns it.

If you feel you must resort to supplements, just make certain they are vegetarian—they certainly are neither raw nor natural. Most large manufacturers provide a small selection of pills specially prepared for vegetarians, but the rest are not. For instance, a non-fish A oil comes from lemon grass oil, and a D from activated ergosterols. But the D, really D2, is the same as in irradiated milk, which may be a possible cause of calcification and cancer. Get your D from the summer sun, or sunflower seeds. Vitamin E, of course, comes from wheat, but its gelatin capsule comes from animals. Buy the liquid; it's half the price.

But enough tablet talk. Since the common carnivorism is of flesh rather than organs, the wisely chosen vegetarian diet, raw or cooked, provides more vitamins and minerals per gram of protein. Disregarding stilbesterol and cholesterol, nitrates and nitrites, vermination and putrefaction, maybe the case is not so much that flesh is all that bad; rather that plant food, consisting of so much more than just protein, is all the better. Than "more" makes the difference between health and illness, and between life and death.

Your last question, unnumbered, is the most important. You ask: *Will you list any qualifications you might have?* My single greatest credential is my health. In examples begin persuasions: I am the healthiest person I know. As I have found what is right for myself, you must find for yourself. Every time I sit in the subway, no more than one or two of the eight or nine people seated opposite me looks healthy, and of those who look healthy no one knows how many actually are. I sincerely hope the others are not as unhealthy as they appear. But health is not an end in itself but a means to an end. And it is a means to postpone the final end.

Herbivorously,

4. Traveling Fast

What, then, do I wish to say? That in order to be moral, people must cease to eat meat? Not at all. I only wish to say that for a good life a certain order of good deeds is indispensable; that if a man's aspirations toward right living be serious, it will inevitably follow one definite sequence; and that in this sequence the first virtue a man will strive after will be temperance, self-renunciation. And in seeking to be temperate a man will inevitably follow one definite sequence, and in this sequence the first thing will be temperance in food, fasting. And in fasting, if he be really and seriously seeking to live a good life, the first thing from which he will abstain will always be the use of animal food, because, to say nothing of the excitation of the passions caused by such food, its use is simply immoral, as it involves the performance of an act which is contrary to the moral feeling—killing.

LEO TOLSTOY
"The First Step"

Fire!

Not enough time for both, you must rescue either your spouse or your sibling. Who would you choose? (What you really should have chosen is between a brick house and a home of wood.) Suppose the choice is between your mate or your life; you are less indecisive. And suppose between your spouse and a lamb, or between his or her leg and a leg of lamb; the answers are clearer here. Now consider your life or a hundred lives of lambs; here we approach closer to our subject. Vegetarianism, however, is not deciding between your life and an animal; but simply whether to shorten and torture the lives of about fifteen cattle, ten sheep, twenty-five hogs, one thousand birds, and one thousand fish: these are the rounded-off numbers of rounded-up animals an ill-rounded American inattentively devours in an average life span, and we won't add up the cows milked dry and the chickens who only count their eggs but never hatch them.

Nonvegetarians posit this notion: once starving for nearly a month, would you eat a rabbit? This dilemma passes from hypothesis to artifice for two reasons. The first is that such people

43

more than likely are urbanites: they work at worrying as an extension of their living in fear. They dwell where nature is nothing more than cats and rats and mice and lice; in resorting to rabbits for food, they forget about the food from which the rabbit came; they would eat anything that moved, and maybe only things that moved. Yet just as more kinds of vegetables than cuts of meat can be bought at a market, more edible plants than capturable animals can be sought on a mountain.

The second reason ignores the premises of the first altogether, because the person before starvation and the one during are not the same: vegetarians do resort to carnivorism just as in the same situations carnivores turn into cannibals. The question is how often these situations occur, and the answer is, hardly often enough to consider it. Only when we walk into the movie theater do we enter such Dark Ages: in "The Gold Rush," when the starved Mack Swain hallucinated Charlie Chaplin into a chicken, that was no joke.

The state of starvation varies from person to person. Picture two people stranded on a barren island. One might begin a fast at the same time that the other would begin to starve, so the first would live for two months while the other would survive for only two weeks. As undeniable as it is unendurable, though the two merge in actions and motions, they vary in reactions and emotions. All matters differ to different minds, and many diseases are only in the mind. Most suffering is an affliction not by a virus but by something just as unexplainable, a desire. In this instance the desire for food kills before the lack of food. The starved hunter, gun in hand, wants to eat, but is unable; one who is fasting is able, but wants not. The former for no reason is forced; the other is voluntary and for a real reason.

But more important than mere reasons are causes. A person fasting as a protest or for a cause can endure far more than someone fasting for health. The person living for a cause and an ideal, indeed the ideal cause, lives forever; ideals and the ideas of those ideals are eternal. We are born to give birth to children and/or to give birth to brain children which our or others' children will keep alive after we die. The one ideal cause is not yet known, but a very good cause among a thousand very good causes is vegetarianism. Thus, given only rabbits to eat, a vegetarian might fast for a very good cause.

The uninitiated assume that fasting, if it is good at all, is good only for the cause; fasters know more, they know it is equally good for their health. An Indian fasted to protest British occupation of India, an American to protest American intervention in Vietnam, and both fasted to dislodge wasteful matters from their bodies and in turn from their troubled minds. Both armies were overwhelming, but not much had to be freed from the fasters' bodies nor much unburdened from their minds: Gandhi was and Dick Gregory is vegetarian.

Here we will see how vegetarianism and fasting are a pair together, and how the person who is serious about one must do the other. For fasting stands to gluttony as vegetarianism stands to carnivorism. Some fast to contest an otherwise incurable disease. That is fine and good. Others fast to protest an injustice across the seas. For these, so long as they are attentive to a few rules, the consequence is not just in heaven but in health.

But let us be realistic. Few causes demand the devotion of an entire life, few forests are large enough that we might be lost in their midst for weeks, and few fires rage where we are forced to choose between our sibling and our spouse. This third most archetypal dilemma involving the right to leave someone to the flames is the most absurd and least likely to occur. It is another thing to throw someone onto the flames: but this is just what is commonly done to animals. Forgetting forests and fires, we had better remember factory farms.

It is improbable that we will ever have to search on hands and knees for food in the gravel, or be forced to sleep in fields and trees when we travel; we will travel by train or plane and sleep in motels or hotels. We will have to search, not for meat, but only for some fresh fruit or whole grain bread. No one eats as well away from home as at home. On a short trip we might pack along our own food, but on longer excursions a wee bit of white sugar here, a morsel of white bread there, a few drops of white milk, and even a few drips of white lard all somehow manage to intrude their way onto the plate and in front of the path.

The detour is greatest if on a longer tour, say of Europe. On such journeys the strength of our vegetarianism truly comes to the test. In Southern Italy, for example, whole wheat pasta is fed only to the sick and dying, the only ones willing to squander an extra lira for a minute more, though, to be fair, in all of Italy a third of the bread is whole grain and salt-free. A hundred years ago only the rich could afford white food; now that the cycle has come half circle, we might instead cross the Alps to Switzerland, where whole-kernel bread outsells white, where the healthy are very healthy, but where the rich are very rich. Typically, in Zurich we find Europe's largest and most luxurious vegetarian restaurant, and also its most expensive. Though health is our greatest wealth, should the wealthy be the only ones healthy?

Instead of eating out, we can either not go out or not eat. The first alternative is a restriction on our lives, but the second is a great freedom. Vegetarian restaurants are not everywhere. Eventually we would eat out of the ordinary sordid greasy spoon. But patronizing is compromising, so travelers should fast simply to protest silently the large numbers of charcoal-broil charnel houses. That the protest is silent is no coincidence. The "word fast" is analogous to the food fast: indeed some shut their mouths to speech at the same time as to sustenance. Pythagoras required his disciples to fast forty days before admitting them under his tutelage. This was before they could hear anything, much less say anything. Christ fasted forty days before he began to preach. Anaxarchus, the Greek philosopher, was tortured by Nicocreon, the King of Cyprus, to betray the names of fellow conspirators, but instead of talking bit out his tongue and spit it in the tyrant's face. He did this after not having eaten for many days. Monks' fasts are as well known as their taciturnity: Trappists are silent; Buddhists, Jains, Benedictines, Carthusians, and Trappists are vegetarians, just about all of them fast; and the majority who speak, speak softly.

This is all serious, yet may seem somewhat mysterious to the person who has never fasted. When fasting, normally obscure and unnoticed stimuli are magnified into either very repulsive or very attractive sights, sounds, smells, and tactile sensations—because the all too overwhelming taste buds have been set to rest. The blind person, and to a lesser and more momemtary degree the blindfolded person, develops keener hearing to compensate for lost sight. Likewise, after a fast, food tastes better than ever before. Even during the fast, mountain spring water could prove to be the most delicious of all meals. On the other hand, bad smells could become so offensive that we would break the fast to be no longer vulnerable to them, particularly to flesh oxidizing in an oven. But the most disturbing of all obstructions is noise so loud that even our shouts for silence go unheard. Here speech fasting is necessary. We shut up. We want to say "Shut Up!" Instead, we set the example; simply and purely and silently, we ourselves shut up.

An entire day could be spent traveling through the cornfields of Illinois without once seeing any cattle for whose mouths the corn is meant. Another entire day could be devoted to roaming through the cattle country of Texas without once seeing any humans for whose mouths the cattle are meant. That is all a great waste of space, where trees once grew in Illinois or could someday be cultivated in Texas. But then, the trees would probably be milled into paper, most of which is also a great waste of space.

Few new books are good because most good books are no longer new. The same is true for books on food, and for food itself: fruits and vegetables were created before animals and humans, but even flesh foods are older than breads, cakes, pies, and fries. We do better reading good books than none, but also no books than bad. The same is truer for books on food and truest for food itself: better to eat nothing that is food than food that is nothing.

Mere reading is in itself of little value. Some read only because they are unable to think for themselves. Worse, the author's thought passes through them unassimilated because they have never stopped to contemplate, but just read on like a tired driver steering through a beautiful landscape, intent on seeing only the distant destination. Worst, some choose authors precisely because of their books' poverty of thought. Readers can be compared to eaters, bestseller lists to quick, but hardly quickening, foods. Proper digestion of the food's total nutrition becomes impossible because most people do not thoroughly chew and then hardly give their stomachs a rest before stuffing it anew.

This is said with the gross assumption that good in the food is to be gotten; quite the contrary, just as people often employ language not to express thoughts but to conceal that they have none, the rotting boxes and rusting cans on the supermarket shelves are adorned with bright colors and beguiling slogans to hide the fact that the packages have nothing in them. (Consequently, people develop all sorts of digestive deficiency diseases, such as colitis and diverticulitis. A bland diet of the very foods which caused the illnesses is prescribed by their doctors, the bland leading the bland. Had the patients fasted instead, they would be giving both themselves and their doctors long needed rests.) Where nothing is put in, nothing can be gotten out. No deposit, no return.

Exhaling is possibly more important than inhaling, and at times fasting is more important than eating.

Such times certainly include when we are away from home. No greater effort is needed to eat a vegetable food than a flesh food, a nourishing food than a junk food, so long as we are at home. Anywhere else, excuses substitute for choices. Everyone must eat, but must not always eat.

The human body is too imperfect to live its whole life fasting. We have no need for pretenses: we are only human. Information and revelation concerning what our humanity really means could very well come from museums and libraries, but more than likely it must come from within. Many sages throughout the ages have said that the answers to our questions will come, if they come at all, through contemplation and fasting. And all questions amount to one: What are we?

If we are what we eat, then we must ask: What do we eat? And from where does what we eat come? Our food either comes directly from plants, or from animals who come from plants. In either case, we indirectly come from what plants directly come from, so we are really eating the sun, the earth, the stars, and the moon. Most of all, plants depend upon the sun—so the sun is most of all that which we really come from. If only we might depend solely upon the sun! Though green with envy, we are not green with chlorophyll. As far as we can see, the sun is the one source to which we owe existence. The ancients, who worshipped the sun since they could see little past it and scarcely into it, knew from where they came; but we seem to have forgotten. We see only that we came from the ancients, so we deify them instead: for instance, Abraham, Moses, Jesus, Zoroaster, Buddha, and Muhammad. And whereas the ancients assumed the first persons born were the stars and the planets, we refer to them under the pseudonyms of Adam and Eve.

The few sun worshippers who still dwell among us can be discerned by a darker tone of summer skin. But they are a bit confused, possibly from sunstroke; they have mistaken a symbol for an entire religion. This is like marrying and forever after happily kissing only the wedding ring. What they really worship is not the sun but their bodies, just as some worship the temple but not the gods within it.

Despite their confused intentions and mixed reactions, the sun shines its blessing upon them day after long hot summer day. This is made manifest by their eating less at summer meals when the transfer of sun energy to food matter to human energy is most direct: they get nourishment straight from the source, sun energy to human energy, without the interception—and consequent energy loss in the conversion—of plants. Yet they could sit all day beneath the sun and need only a few less mouthfuls of food. That is how inefficient we all are at transforming energy.

We could actually expose ourselves to too much sun and lose our heads over it, just as eating too much food makes us lose our bodies. Indeed, we need sun-nourished plants not merely for food but also for shade, else our Icarian wings melt and plunge us into the vast sea of indifference.

Shade is one thing, darkness quite another. A plant, whose leaves are mirrors angled to the sun, is a reflection of the light from which it feeds; but animals who feed on reflections are shade and shadows; and animals who feed on shadows are darkness. No true Daedalus among us should be so foolish as to try to see the light by eating an eviscerated corpse drained of life. Like the tax collector who expends ninety-nine cents to expunge a dollar, the carnivore, losing much of what was gathered along the way, indulges in a waste of energy demanding a four-fold transformation: one, sun energy to plant matter; two, plant matter to animal matter; three, animal matter to human matter; four, human matter to human energy. This pervasive unwillingness to gather one's plants for oneself but, rather, to depend upon a cow or a pig or a chicken to do it, is due to society's aggregate equivalent of individual laziness and selfishness. Growing garden plants, gathering them by hand, creating them into meals at home, are all concerns for humble people who wish to do as many chores for themselves as possible. Enough to depend upon plants, we can excuse our dependence also on farmers; but who can justify the ultimate services of a cow or a pig or a chicken?

Rudolf Steiner, in "Problems of Nutrition," posits that when eating plants, humans are compelled to do a lot of internal work themselves because plants do not manufacture fat. The vegetarian human body thus must produce fat of its own, an activity otherwise spared when consuming the ready-made fat of flesh food. He believed vegetarians are lords and creators of their bodies, but carnivores, by passing on the task of fat formation to the animals they eat, remain mere spectators and forestall their own spiritual growth. We might deduce from this that the whole phenomenon of spirituality boils down to the question of energy, that spirit is the essence of energy which animates, and that the greater we are spiritually developed the more we are self-animated. It is no coincidence that the Christian day of worship falls on "Sunday."

*   *   *

Whether it is the light or the warmth from the sun that is most needed is unclear. A tomato plant, of course, depends upon sunlight for growth, but a tomato can ripen in a dark room when warm. This much is certain: those regions on the earth's surface which are warmest also receive the most direct light. Of all plants, trees with their thousands of leaves gather the most light; of all fruits from trees, tropical fruits from latitudes of fewest degrees are the "lightest." Excluding severe hypoglycemics, the exceptions who prove the rule, all our diets would benefit from an increase in fruits, and particularly in tropical fruits. Of all fruits the mango is just about the sweetest, the papaya the most soothing, and the avocado probably the most nutritious. Eskimos, to whom fruits from trees are hardly forbidden but simply unavailable, are known for their short lives. This could be as much due to the flesh they eat as to the fruits they do not eat.

Fruits contain the greatest concentration of sun energy in the least amount of space. We in turn need the least exertion of our own energy to assimilate that plant matter into human matter: fruits generally require less than an hour to be digested, fruit juices twenty minutes, as opposed to four hours for flesh. In all fairness, unsoaked nuts take four hours too; yet soaked nuts, requiring an hour, become more like fruits. And the opposite is true: dried fruits are closer to nuts and need four hours. So, we soak nuts and dried fruits before eating them.

The foods to eat just before and just after a fast are fruits. This parodies the classic form of the sonata, as in a Beethoven quartet: ACA. Fruits are the foods nearest to juice just as fruit juices are the liquids nearest to water. Far more gradual, and therefore more effective transitions occur when surrounding the days of fasting by days of fruit juices, and of fruit juices by fruits. Here we hear, if we have the ear, the particular "andante" movement in Op. 132 offered as a prayer of holy thanksgiving for recovery from a nearly fatal illness: ABCBA. Clearly, traveling fast is best accompanied in priority and posteriority by eating lightly.

Life-long fasters who have practiced various techniques and studied the experiences of their peers and their forebears, nearly unanimously agree that the best whole food upon which to break a fast is fruit, while absolutely no one prefers flesh. Eating flesh, or pizza, or cake, or fries is bad enough, but it is worse to eat them as the last meal preceding or the first following a fast. Alternatively, fasting can be undertaken precisely because such a meal has been eaten; this strategy ignores all else and employs the fast as a defense solely for its cleansing effects. But fruits best break fasts: those which flush through the body with the greatest of ease are melons, plums, grapes, and the blackest cherries. Flesh, however, will clog the flow like mortar in the hole of a dam, and as the mortar dries to the consistency of concrete walls, the waters will grow more polluted. We should note that frankfurters and cold cuts are already made of intestinal walls, so it is no wonder they would clog our own.

Fasting metaphorically turns the human body upside-down and inside-out; what go inside-out are the toxins, and upside-down are the intestines. Though nothing is eaten, much waste is eliminated. Even those who maintain a healthful diet walk around with five pounds of feces; a first fast of three days will be the most effective means of discarding it, and fairly regular fasts thereafter will keep both the pounds off and the feces out.

Although eating fruit is less an effort than eating flesh, eating nothing is the least of all efforts. Nothing is easier than not doing; it may be difficult to begin again to do the thing left long undone. Fasting is easy, breaking the fast hard. The first fast, however, is the most troublesome and painful because of what comes out, while the first day of eating after any fast can be catastrophic precisely because of what does not come out. No strain is necessary to eat nothing, but after breaking the fast more effort is needed to eat little than to eat a lot. The worst thing we can do is gorge ourselves, like a liberated Tantalus maddened by hunger.

A modified form of fasting is a lengthy diet of just fruit juices. Some eat whole fruits and consider that a kind of fast too. The implication should be obvious. Every argument defending carnivorism can be extended to periodic cannibalism—particularly cannibalism upon enemies in times of war—in the same manner that any proposition favoring vegetarianism extends to periodic fasting. Likewise, factors in favor of fasting extend to vegetarianism. Vegetarians who eat especially large quantities of fruit need hardly fast and need hardly be concerned about the task of breaking it when they do. Fewer toxins are excreted because fewer are eaten. The opposite of fruit is flesh: Arnold Ehret warns carnivores to fast with great caution since humans' own toxins are already too much; the stampede of the animals' as well could do a lot of harm before doing a lot of good.

Ehret may not have been the record-breaker of our century's fasters but is probably the most well-known. He also knew very well what he was doing. What must be emphasized is that he knew what he was doing for himself, and for himself alone. As with eating, knowledge concerning abstention from eating must be found out for ourselves. Who would not rather experience life for himself than read the conjectures of a hundred philosophers and the exegeses of a hundred thousand professors of philosophy? Most important, after finding out about fasting for ourselves, we will find out alot about ourselves.

When we eat, the body directs energy to digestion, to overcome food to make it become ourselves. But when we fast, energy can instead be directed to making us become more ourselves. We look into the mirror and do not recognize our faces; we think and do not recognize our thoughts; we speak and do not recognize our voices. We become persons other than normally known, persons otherwise hidden deep within. But we are not transformed, nor are our old selves forgotten; rather, our conception of our old selves is forgotten; we suddenly see and hear as though for the first time. The stupor of the first fasts is difficult, but compensated for by the vigor of the first days after them.

Now our question must be, "How to fast?" Techniques vary. For some, eating only apples is a fast, while for others it is drinking only apple juice. Some say it is imperative to drink some kind of fresh fruit juice, others to drink herb teas with honey and lemon. Some designate fasting as drinking only water and specify spring water because the distilled kind drains the body of minerals. Others say to drink distilled water precisely because those minerals are the inorganic deposits for which the body has no use. Some recommend continuing the fast until the tongue clears, others until hunger reappears. Some assert the necessity of enemas, others condemn them except in the most extreme emergencies.

It is easy to see that the science of abstention from nourishment is as confusing as that of obtaining it. We can ignore the whole matter and choose never to fast, though this is comparable to developing an aversion to drinking water because of an inability to swim. This much must be construed: we are as wise to ignore those books that advise how not to eat but not how to eat as to close our minds to the opposite, those which discuss food but not fasting from food.

In the late 1970s, many fasting books with calligraphic titles and psychedelic covers appeared whose single synonym for the subject was "weight loss." These books, written by and for average carnivores, appeared almost overnight and disappeared as quickly. We whose concerns are nutritional and not cosmetic must be vigilant to discern the quick from the dead. Like figs and dates, which are as appetizing aged as fresh, the serious books on fasting have remained in print for years; and the three best are not coincidentally but absolutely an essential part of a larger system of diet and living. The first, Arnold Ehret's 1922 *Mucusless Diet Healing System* should be read before the first fast; the second is Paul Bragg's *The Miracle of Fasting*, best read during the fast; *Fasting for the Renewal of Life* by Herbert Shelton is the third, which should be consulted for any developments, usually good but sometimes bad, during and after the fast. Their emphasis is on fasting as a part of a sane system of vegetarian eating; they speak equally of sustenance, not just abstinence.

Those books, good and bad, whether written for the health of readers or the wealth of writers, need not be read for us to discover their differences. A glance is enough: we can tell a health book by its back cover. The meritorious, serious fasting books display photographs of their authors (unless they intend to perpetuate their obscurity), whose pictures of health promote their contents. The meretricious, fake fasting books dare not exhibit their authors, who often have too much to hide. Of fad books that do picture the author, the most notorious is liquid animal protein advocate Linn, shown aiming a fat finger at an unseen target like Moses pointing to the promised land into which he is forbidden entry.

This is the case of almost all health books by doctors of traditional allopathic medicine. One who looks neurotic writes on overcoming nervousness; another who is growing bald writes on healthy hair; a third who chain smokes writes on physical fitness. True, too, for pill nutritionists, such as the well known vitamin therapist who died of cancer. Traditional medicine opposes traditional nutrition, but fasting and vegetarianism contradict them both. Meanwhile, all health services and nutritional advice contrary to allopathic medicine are considered heresy to the law of the land of hospitals and slaughterhouses and must be administered accompanied by an obligatory caveat.

It hardly occurs to the polluted and deluded to fast. This is perhaps to be expected. If many had this notion, no delusion would exist: what the deluded most need is what they least perceive or believe. Meanwhile they settle for pills and potions, symbols of and substitutes for what they seek, and as many die from their pills as from their ills. All fasting does is assure the body a chance to cure itself; yet after a fast already healthy people will feel even healthier, and those who eat judiciously and fast regularly can feel better after a week without food than the week before.

Why? The Greek gods dined on ambrosia and nectar, but our every mouthful reminds us of our mortality. For the cast-iron pot, we give up an iron stomach, and end up with a pot belly. Humanity, bulbous-bellied but still its eyes bigger than its mouth, will never return to peace with its gods by saying grace at any dinner table. Fruit alone will not even help; the apple was the problem in the first place.

The fasts of Western religions last only one day, as in Judaism, or only during the day, as in Islam, or only from one food, as in Christianity. Fasting for only a day is just long enough to begin to feel hunger, but not long enough for its gnawing to subside, as will happen by the second or certainly third day. Even when not fasting, healthful eaters and frequent fasters rarely experience hunger; hunger is an ill omen, a nudge in the ribs to remind sufferers of lives gone wrong. A forgotten meal or first fasting day should only cause a funny feeling in the throat. But try telling this to someone on the first day of the first fast! Initiates will need more than just assurances; they will need faith. As for seeing gods, instead they will see only a lot of mucus, feces, and even vomit. Determination to persist beyond the first day of hunger, the second day possibly of dizziness, and perhaps a third day of nausea, is of no consequence if we are unprepared for the final day of reckoning, the day we break the fast. Wrongly turning to inappropriate foods means nothing is gained, and something is even lost.

Along with the leap of faith, the sweep of faith is needed: the sweep of the intestines, not just the intentions. The leap loosens the mental strait-jacket in which even the most rational wrap themselves, while the sweep loosens the bowels. Following the leaping and sweeping comes the reaping: after the intestines are cleared of waste, we who maintain a whole and mostly raw diet will no longer need nutrients in the gross amounts specified by government bureaucrats. Unlike our own, the heavy-meat and sugar-sweet diet of complicated cookery and simplistic food-combining (which simply combines everything) necessitates ridiculous recommendations for numberless nutrients merely to cut through the almost impenetrable digestive system, stuck with muck.

The case of B12 illustrates this point precisely. Researchers recommend their dosages for the typical consumer of lots of fat and protein from lots of flesh and milk, as well as lots of nothing from lots of white food. But they are blind guides leading a blind tribe. Flesh and milk, the most often cited sources of the vitamin, have also the most saturated fats: deficiencies develop in laboratory animals fed normal amounts of B12 with high amounts of fat. Similarly, high animal protein diets deplete the vitamin, and diets dominated by white foods double the B12 required by baboons. (These are insights already adduced by vegetarians, but it took the sufferings of thousands of animals to knock this into the skulls of scientists. Plumbers of pipes may know more than probers of pulsars and certainly surgeons of stomachs, that is, grease clogs drains.) Humans who eat only whole plant foods need far less of the vitamin than cooked-food carnivores need. And humans who fast, drink no alcohol, smoke no tobacco, and eat only whole raw plant foods most likely produce for themselves all they need. B12 or not B12: that is the question.

Until we fast, all reasoning concerning it supports opinion but does not prove it; its merits will remain hard to defend and difficult to understand. But once we have put the horse of experience in front of the cart of rationality, excessive needs for nutrients are not the only extraneous things eliminated. The desire for food disappears after the first day of a fast, and other desires disappear later. For instance, after about three days we might walk past the store window that displays that new coat eyed so enviously for weeks, but today winter will seem very far away and we will remember our other three coats, two more than we need.

By the fifth day, all sexual impulses for moonlight liasons eclipse into evanescence and become moonlight sonatas. Gandhi rarely discussed fasting without mentioning celibacy. Wooing and eating and drinking are pleasures undeniably, but not undeniable; be they as they may, they are pleasures only of the body. Denying sex and food and drink are also pleasures—of the soul.

Desires are cast behind not just during fasts but, if fasts are regularly conducted, between them as well. If one has not done so, vegetarianism will surely be embraced. While Moses fasted for forty days and forty nights the first time atop Mount Sinai, his people were worshipping a calf which, lucky for the calf, was made of gold instead of flesh and blood. Seeing this, Moses realized his generation was not ready for a new life. So he fasted for another forty days and forty nights, awaiting new instructions. Then for forty years he led a pilgrimage in the desert until new generations grew new bodies; only with that were they prepared for their new lives. The wandering was a sort of fast in preparation for an entrance into a new land.

The carnivore converting to vegetarianism, the vegetarian to veganism, the vegan to raw foods, would all more assuredly topple the obstacles along life's way if they fasted during their steps into new lands. Their fasts would detoxify them over a quick period of days, instead of their new diets doing so over months, and no one could mistakenly attribute to their new vegetarian diet the sickness that comes from cleansing. This is important: the neophyte's nausea does not come directly from vegetarianism or from fasting. Rather, nausea comes from cleansing; it is the cleansing that comes directly from vegetarianism or from fasting. Those who complain of tiredness and headache during their first month of vegetarianism blame their ills on doing without flesh food rather than on having done with it for so long. Quick to chop off the head of the messenger who brings bad news, they revert to carnivorism and continue chopping off a lot of other heads.

If we ignore all bad news, it will cease to be given to us. Sychophants to sickness are impatient: willing to try everything once, they rarely try anything twice. It is easy to pack for a new home if we have never unpacked from our old one, and those ready to depart for a new land on a moment's notice usually never had a home from the start. For the rest of us, house-cleaning must precede house-moving. Dumping wasteful baggage which should never have accumulated in the first place makes more sense than dragging it along to the second. Old habits are as much embedded in the mind as old feces in the intestines. Too many people accept both as part of life. But what kind of life is that? It is that of the man who carried a chair wherever he went so that whenever he wearied he could sit on it. He felt grateful for the chair, yet never realized that carrying it was what made him so tired.

Fully a year is necessary for initiates to judge any diet's impact, but if the first month is endured, then abstinence is bound to last. Fasting facilitates graceful transitions, not just bodily but spiritually: such is the true mark both of all abstinence and all sustenance. Gandhi grew spiritually so intensely in his later life that he fasted as many days as he ate; when he did eat he limited his menu to five items a day, and never ate after sunset or before sunrise. His mind was elsewhere than on food, or perhaps it was on everything at once: not just on what grows under the sun but with all that glows above it.

A stage could eventually be reached when fasting is no longer necessary. Toxins, always produced in metabolism, should be no more than the healthy body is capable of expelling. A few years of periodic fasting should rid the body of the old load, and a regular raw vegetarian diet should forbid any new one. A sign that the body is renewed is sudden difficulty in fasting, which previously was easy. The negative proof of this is the sick who lose appetite despite the tea and chicken soup in which they drown and the aspirin and antibiotics which they down. Those who constantly and easily fast probably need to do so until, though they still wish to do so, it no longer is so easy. So an umbilical tie is severed, and the fast becomes a part of the past.

*   *   *

We all need green. It is a metaphysical if not medical fact that no color renders rest so immediately to its viewer. Chlorophyll is green, thus leaves are green, thus trees are green, thus forests are green. Where climates are coldest, where winters are whitest, leaves stay green year round. Suburbanites grow gardens as hobbies, and even city dwellers cultivate house plants by their soot-stained windows to compensate for what they do not see outside. But a woodsman, whose home is made of the very trees surrounding his cabin needs no windows.

One reason the American urban populace is so frenetic is that its diet of fried foods, white foods, and flesh foods is particularly high in phosphorus, disturbing the balance of calcium and magnesium, which in turn causes nervousness: mineral imbalance is but a step toward mental imbalance. Another instigating factor is that it rarely sees green, so "loses its cool" and "sees red" which opposes green on the color wheel. And what is cholorophyll? The substance found outside the body that is most nearly identical to the hemoglobin inside. They differ chemically only in that, where iron is found in hemoglobin, magnesium constitutes chlorophyll; chromatically, blood is red, while leaves are green. Complementary colors create harmony in our homes. Likewise in our more inner interiors. Those who see green least have a greater cause for eating it. And the best greens are the sprouts and seedlings of our indoor window-sill and kitchen-cabinet gardens. They almost grow themselves. These are the cleanest, freshest, and indeed the greenest of any vegetables that even land-owning urbanites can hope to obtain: outdoors, city gardens are full of lead—as though shot by bullets—and of fall-out—as though bombed by nuclear arms—yet the wars waged are usually against insects, sometimes against rodents, and only occasionally against neighbors.

Rarely having enough chance to see green, city people should eat less flesh: their own bodies are red enough. The more red flesh eaten, the more are green vegetables needed to match. Hence bottomless salad bowls frequently accompany mistaken main courses at steak houses. Farmers and woodsmen, who not only grow their own green but kill their own red, can get along eating flesh better than can urbanites. Just as painting masters mix their own paints from pigments (often of the very land they live on, called earth colors), carnivores who endeavor to view a clear picture of reality should spill the blood of the animals they live on. Those who ignore mineral balances, color harmonies, and moral imperatives should forewarn others. For instance, if they were to affix on their cars the bumper sticker "Warning: I Breakfast on Animals," others might know to steer clear of their peers reared on steer.

Chlorophyll benefits everyone, not just the carnivore. Some get by eating few greens by eating no reds. Fruits comprise all the colors in between, and again take position alongside sprouts as the opposite of flesh: a fruit generally ripens from green to red, while no-nitrate flesh putrefies from red to green. The only truly green "fruit-fruit" is the avocado, the platypus of plants, nutritionally more like a vegetable and digestibly more like a nut. Another fruit nearly as green is the lime, which goes very well with the avocado.

Food-combination and protein-complement charts could probably be drawn according to color alone. In fact, a whole healing discipline uses color as its basic criterion for what to eat. But older than chromotherapy is healing by fasting, whose diet consumes no color: clear water and clean air are both colorless. Those who fast in cities should do so on weekends when factories are closed and traffic is thin, and drink spring or distilled water, though they might resort to the faucet at other times. Clear fruit juices and herb teas can be indulged in by the faster, since these are translucent as opposed to opaque.

The interaction of colors relates to fasting in far stranger ways. When a painter mixes all the colors on the palette, no matter how intense the yellow or deep the blue or bright the red, it all comes out a dull brown. The same for eating, for mixing all the colors under the palate, no matter how green the spinach or red the raspberry or yellow the lemon or orange the orange or even white the flour and the sugar, it too all comes out a dull brown. Were the fasting process merely material, nothing would come out where nothing was put in; quite the contrary, color has as much to do with not eating as with eating. Bowels still will move, but instead of the brown color from mixing everything, the absence of food shows the absence of color: black.

Black is associated with the opposite of white, white being the color of light, and light being the essence of life. This is a great reason for fasting only once if we never fast again, for it is on the first fast that we get out the most black. We have already observed that in conjunction with a raw vegetarian diet, fasting can be superfluous: the death of a plant amounts to less than the death of an animal. The rare people who subsist solely on fruits never need fast since their diet is full of life and light, not death and darkness.

Lumberjacks catch neither Chestnut nor Dutch Elm Disease, and farmers are immune to the blights to which their crops succumb. But many illnesses in the chicken coop are contagious to their keepers; a tubercular cow transmits her bacteria through raw milk, and trichinosis is communicable to anyone who brings home the bacon. The lower along the twisted chain of life from which we eat, the less incidence of disease we receive from our food. Fasting extends these ends so far down the line that we bend below it, escape it, and transcend it.

The scale of eaten animal life to human life registers as one day more of animal eating equaling one day less of human living. Such a system of subtraction carries no place for addition; that is the measure where fasting makes its mark. Every day fasted is an extra day of life, for as far as the body's metabolism is concerned, a day of rest from the toils of digestion is a day not lived. Thus the average person who fasts just a day a week should live eighty years, not just seventy. Proof of this need not be sought in any library stack, livery stable, or operating table. All we need to do is listen to the beats of our own hearts: pulse rates lower with each day of fasting, as with animals in hibernation. Clues become keys, keys become knowledge—so long as we have found the door of disquisition. The pulse is the clue, the body is the key, health is the door, and through long life comes knowledge. We all are born with keys to happiness, but are left to our own devices in finding our proper doors.

The Bible warns that he who does not fast cannot enter the kingdom of heaven, while it would have been safer to say that one way among many ways of achieving eternal life is through fasting. But it has been "only" long life, not eternal life, about which we have here spoken, and then only in token. Eve's temptation of the apple is a parable of gluttony, a sin from which other little sins and other little Adams and little Eves sprout and stem. Noah should have fasted for those forty days and forty nights while tossing upon the sea of wrath, but instead turned the ark into a cupboard and brought food along for everybody.

This must have meant fodder for lambs, lambs for lions, and fodder and lambs for Noah. Though never attributing it to his dereliction of duty, only beginning with Noah does the Bible mention human carnivorism.

To Adam was given "every plant yielding seed" and "every tree with seed in its fruit"; but Noah got "every moving thing that lives." From Noah onward, the stench of burning flesh became a "pleasing odor" to the Lord, and animals fell into categories of those to be sacrificed and those not, those to be eaten and those not, and the four more permutations of their own combinations. And before Noah, people lived to 700 and 900 years old (Methuselah to 969); but after Noah they lived to only 120 and 150. Whether an ancient year was shorter than our own is not what we must most immediately put to question; what we must ask is whether a life of flesh eating is shorter than of fruit eating.

All things considered, a remaining question is "Why does everyone not fast?" And a correlate, "Why is everyone not a vegetarian?" We will unfortunately disregard the first, leave until later the second, and have to be content with having addressed ourselves to a third question "Why does every vegetarian not fast?" An objection has sometimes been raised by vegetarians that fasting is an extreme form of carnivorism, a self-cannibalism. Shame on vegetarians for casting doubt on such a useful tool and its many toolmakers when they should be instead denigrating the likes of Frank Perdue, Oscar Mayer, and Colonel Sanders!

Once upon a time, a city supermarket Daniel Boone meant to kill a chicken but slipped and instead of the head he chopped off his own hand. Since he was as hungry for something on his plate as the chicken was hasty to make its escape, he quickly figured that if he could eat pig's knuckles he might as well eat his own knuckles. Instead of a ham sandwich he prepared a hand sandwich, like Harpo Marx spreading mustard not on the hot dog but on the hot dog vendor, biting into his hand between two slices of bread. The next day, recalling his mother's recipe for fried chicken handed down from generation to generation in his old Kentucky home, he dipped the leftover in batter, shook the hand in bread crumbs, and fried it in chicken fat. "They snatch on the right, but are still hungry; and they devour on the left, but are not satisfied; each devours the flesh of his arm . . . and his hand is stretched out still" (Isaiah 9.20–21).

Chicken-Fried Kentuckian.

5. The Milky Way

Those who lament over the barbarism that comes out of barbarism are like people who wish to eat their veal without slaughtering the calf. They are willing to eat the calf, but they dislike the sight of blood. They are easily satisfied if the butcher washes his hands before weighing the meat.

BERTOLT BRECHT
"Writing the Truth:
Five Difficulties"

Writing exists at once *for* those who read, and *against* those who do not read. If you have read thus far, the preceding was probably for you; but if you believe you drink your milk "without slaughtering the calf," the following shall be against you. However, mere writing and reading neither postulate nor prove a thing. We have to remember that much of what we read concerning what to eat is written by those who do not hesitate to lie through their typewriter teeth if either themselves or their rulers—merchants not monarchs—stand to gain a profit from it. And even where something relatively truthful is told, it is often by those neither old enough nor bold enough to put it into practice.

The West at once possesses the tallest and most durable houses of worship, yet the greatest and most destructive warships and the largest and most efficient slaughterhouses. Bad enough to kill; worse to harm and then kill; worst to harm, to continue harming, and yet not kill. Some suffering can be so great that killing is almost kind: putting the soul out of its body also means putting the body out of its pain. "Killing" implies immediacy; "harming" denotes slow death. Still, "humane killing," that gross contradiction, can be excusable if every possible effort first to end the suffering has failed. Factory-farming conditions by which most milk and eggs are produced cause great suffering to cows, to their calves, and to chickens. Domastication [sic] of animals compares to slavery of humans, and in place of the few surviving species of animal predators has evolved a whole new race of human creditors, milking them dry.

61

Vegetarians who drink milk or eat cheese and eggs have three choices of change: killing animals, thus stopping the suffering, and eating the flesh, wasting no food (thereby ceasing to be vegetarians); or keeping goats in sheds and chickens in kitchens, thus assuring their well-being, and eating only their milk and eggs, (thereby remaining lacto-ovo-vegetarians); or renouncing milk and eggs altogether (thereby becoming vegans).

Abandoning these animal products also means abandoning their animal producers, but since everyone is not becoming a vegetarian, nor would do so overnight, no one need wait up late at night worrying until the cows come home. Meantime, we should worry that the cows *are* home. The inhumane exploitation of cow and chicken has already been exposed by Peter Singer in *Animal Liberation*, so we can here forego enlisting in the chorus of complaint; but of the cow's calves and the chicken's chicks, something need be said.

First of all, the chickens have no chicks. This is actually an advantage of that industry, though hens might complain of no husbands to peck and of counting their chickens all their lives before they hatch. As long as two-week-old chicks are not considered delicacies from which famous French chefs can carve out magical recipes, and so do not join the ranks of other animal children such as lambs and calves who long ago passed through the gates of the teeth of time and disappeared down the esophagi of eternity, this is one favorable aspect of the egg industry over the milk. Farmers and those they feed argue that factory farming at least brings animals into this world that might otherwise never be snatched from the other. The retort that selfhood is not justifiable at the cost of serfdom and suffering is not yet relevant here, for first we must question whether selfhood can be discussed. If we can discuss existence because we exist, we cannot discuss non-existence precisely because we can discuss existence. Words are shadows of objects; where there is neither sun nor objects, there are no words. We cannot see a fruit if we are blind, nor taste it if we are tongueless; but even with all our senses intact we cannot see, taste, or even talk about an ungrown fruit—or an unborn chick. It is ill-conceived to speak of the unconceived. What if they gave a chicken barbecue and nobody came, not even the chickens?

Because both cow and calf share common stalls, our bovine companions are half as fortunate as our feathered friends. Even in the most loving of circumstances within the small family farm, cows deserve better than what winter's worst brings: barns heated only by their bodies, and walks for but an hour a day. The calves for whom the milk is meant are confined to even less varied and more brutal existences. Humans rob the calves from the cows, and the milk from the calves. Though cows produce enough milk for both humans and calves (for humans have bred them to do that), humans are greedy: all male calves and over half the females are kidnapped in the first week of birth, shipped to the veal farm where they are fattened for half a year, then taken to the slaughterhouse, and to the supermarket—where they fatten humans. Of every five calves born four are for meals of veal. Thus veal floats invisibly in everyone's milk.

Cows must be milked . . . but by the calves for whom the milk is intended. It is often argued that cows would die if left unmilked. Cows would also surely die if left unfed, yet they are fed not because of compassion but because of thirst. Furthermore, since bulls are rarely let loose with cows, the species would perish if it were not artificially inseminated; yet they are conceived not because of conservation but to maintain peak lactation. Milkers' arguments for keeping cows compare with those of hunters' for killing deer: so that they don't starve to death in the winter, many are shot to death in the fall. Years ago deer had natural predators in wolves and bobcats which have been decimated by hunters. Today they conveniently claim they *must* hunt the deer. Pretty explanations for atrocious acts have always been found by societies and cultures, milk cultures included.

What is milk? It is not animal, yet not vegetable either. Mammal young of both carnivores and herbivores drink it, and its nutritional effect is rather close to both flesh and plants. No adult vegetarian would eat a hamburger made half of flesh just because the other half is of extender made from soy beans, yet most vegetarians drink milk. What comes from an animal certainly comes closer to being an animal than what comes from a plant. For the vegetarian, that is too close for comfort; and for the cow confined to her stall and her many calves to their few cages, that also is too close for comfort. Here it should be noted that not only does an egg come from an animal, but it can become an animal.

Lacto-vegetarians generally mix everything eaten "au lait" and often consume more lacteal liquids than do carnivores meat and milk. Yet milk is but blood modified by mammary glands. The Masai bleed their cows at the neck and milk them at the breast, and drink both the blood and the milk. Like monks masturbating, milk-drinking vegetarians are imitating the very thing they wish to avoid. Their lips can be white from milk only because others' hands are red from blood. Jack made no mistake when he traded his cow for a handful of beans (or when he sought the goose whose eggs were not for eating). Cows make milk as food upon which small cows can become big cows; calves are small, but not all things small are calves; because humans are small compared to cows means not that they are calves, yet they strangely try to grow into big cows.

The belief that cows' milk is made as food for humans is as fallacious as the belief that their blood is for humans, and the trail of blood leads directly to the belief that their flesh is made as food for humans: it is flesh from which flows both blood and milk.

Someone might someday market cows' tears, promoting them as a rich source of mineral salts. Inducing cows to shed them should be no problem: they must forever be crying over their spilled milk.

The three foods nature creates solely for the sake of feeding animals are eggs, milk, and honey. Not even fruits fulfill this sole function since they really envelope seeds of propagation, acting as gift wrap around a birthday present, at once a disguise and a cosmetic. Not coincidentally, these three particular foods are made by the three particular animals for whom they are meant. The foodstuff of eggs is laid by the mother bird for the bird embryo also in the egg; milk is secreted by the mother mammal for the infant mammal also delivered from her; and honey, made by bees, is meant for bees. While animals adapt themselves to what they eat, milk and honey adapt themselves to the animals by whom they are meant to be eaten. Thus human milk is specially adapted for humans, kangaroo milk for kangaroos, bat milk for bats . . . and cow milk for cows. Most human babies are born with an innate aversion to cow milk; but some infants immediately yearn for it. This should alert mom and dad that perhaps they mistakenly have given birth to a calf.

Cow milk contains three times more calcium than human milk. Cows develop bones first, for which all the calcium is needed; humans develop brains first. Cows may be less intelligent than people, yet no mother cow is so simple-minded as to substitute human milk for hers. Ever since humans first were humans, their babies have been fed human milk (and that is meant to be); adults have included cow milk as a small part of their diets for several centuries, but only as recently as the last two was it included in their infants' and as a large part at that. Whether this development tells more about the way adults feed themselves, or about the way they feed their chidren, or about the way they feed themselves as though children, is unclear; but we know that milk drinking is a child's way of growing up.

These past two centuries have also seen a sharp increase in adult humans' cow milk consumption and hence production. Because we are now slaves to milk, cows are slaves to us. Slaves earn no vacations, no leaves of absence for maternal affairs. Forced to produce milk at least eleven months a year, a cow's own tissues are depleted so that her milk might ostensibly nourish her calves. Her body becomes diseased; but rather than give her a vacation, humans give her a vaccination. Her milk becomes tubercular but, rather than put her out to pasture, humans pasteurize her milk.

Many people eat everything at hand, including the hand. Those who drink cow milk, and yet permit her mistreatment, are biting that hand that feeds them; those who eat her flesh are eating the hand. But if we bite, or eat, the hand that feeds us, eventually it will stop feeding us or will feed us one last time—with poison. Like the chick within the fertile egg, ethical consequences underlie nutritional considerations. No foods as much as those from animals are so controversial concerning what is unsafe and unholy.

The venerable law of karmic consequence dictates that those who in early life exploit cows and calves, later in life will be plagued by parasites and paralysis. Raw milk is perhaps only half as bad as the sterilized supermarket version, but the stringent controls necessary for an edible raw milk limit its supply drastically. What is gained in quantity, of course, is lost in quality. Modern America guzzles so much on account of pasteurization, a process which not only eliminates the beneficial bacteria along with the bad but destroys vitamins and renders minerals indigestible. Numerous studies link pasteurization, not milk itself, with arthritis. And we need be neither scientists nor statisticians to link its quick-cooking with its hard-drinking.

The factory-bred and conveyor-belt-fed cow today yields more milk yet lives shorter than it did fifty years ago. And its breeders and feeders drink more milk, yet are hardly any healthier. Only

humans suffer from the cholesterol-related diseases of coronary
sclerosis in middle life and atherosclerosis in late life, and only
humans drink milk past early life. Milk is also a great mucus former. Arnold Ehret, an eccentric in some ways, a prophet in
others, contended that mucus is the cause, not the product, of
the common cold. No one knows the cure for the common cold,
but those who neither eat flesh nor drink milk know the prevention.

If we were fortunate to have been breastfed, we were nevertheless weaned from our mother at one or two years of age. What of
those who have yet to be weaned from the cow mother? Who
would believe they departed from childhoods as humans only to
grow into baby cows? Digestion of the mother's lactose, the
sugar in milk, depends on secretion of the child's lactase. The
majority of the non-Caucasian adult world—notably Orientals,
North and South American Indians, and black Africans—cannot
digest, and therefore do not drink, milk. The Chinese raised
cows for centuries, but for the flesh, and ate it sparingly: the
Orientals have gotten flesh and milk from the simple soybean.
Western nutritionists remain unable to explain the predominant
"lactose-intolerance" because they explore the answer in jungles
and deserts. Some propose genetic digestive deficiencies, others
acquired inabilities; the confusion is needless. The ancient Epi-
charmus, who said, "Only the mind can see and hear, everything
else is deaf and blind," must have been deaf and blind. In this
case we should listen with our stomachs. If we withdraw all milk
and milk products from our diets for just one year, we too will
lose our childish abilities to digest milk, outgrowing it as surely
as we outgrew the pacifier and mother's breast.

The thought of bending down on our knees to suck at the tit of
a zebra or a donkey, or lifting up to our mouths the nipple of a
beaver or a monkey, would solicit a response of either laughter or
regurgitation. Why is it any different with a cow, or a goat, or a
sheep? Are we to equate ourselves with the leech, but instead of
sucking blood from the leg of another human we suck milk from
the tit of a cow? Not even the mother cow drinks her own milk.
Such a cow would hardly differ from a man drinking his own
blood, which hardly differs from a cow drinking a woman's milk.
Her calf drinks her milk but she herself does not. Why does the
man? Because he also drinks the calf's blood.

The old story of the UNICEF program which donated truckloads
of dry milk to African children attests to the wisdom of the Third
World—they used it to whitewash walls—as well as to the cul-

tural imperialism and ethnocentrism of the "First." What one race of people digest, disgusts another. Eskimos have been known to devour so much raw flesh at a single sitting that at the end they could not stand up; Northwest American Indians traditionally competed against one another in a variation of their potlatch with salmon as the wealth, and each contestant destroyed by digestion as much as fifteen pounds of it cold; Tartar tribesmen relished frozen horse flesh; and to this very day the French esteem fried frogs' legs and steamed snails. All of this might be regarded by the average American beef-eater as loathsome, yet no carnivores witnessing any of the above can experience half as much revulsion as do vegetarians in viewing their Pepsi generation peers eating beef and burgers.

Those who prefer their beef rare might be impressed by the Abyssinians who drove a cow to the kitchen door, severed chunks of flesh from its still living body, and then engorged greedily while the animal watched from outside. A fisherman once caught a fish, cut a morsel from its side, baited his hook with it, threw the fish back to the water, and then caught the same fish. Not wishing to waste food, the family often feeds its leftover flesh from the suffer [sic] table to the dog or cat. Yet they toss it to the wrong animal and would waste far less giving it back to the animal from which it came: it needs it most. The twice-caught fish obviously lacked something and did its best to retrieve what it once possessed. Those animals who must eat others' bodies do so because of a deficiency, be it nutritional or spiritual. Eating is a means of seeking companionship with the things we eat. Those who eat many animals must be very lonely.

We have our weaknesses. When we want to be treated like everyone else, we say we are also human; but when we want special privileges, we say we are only human. And we are also only animal. As much as we may or may not put animal bodies into our mouths, our mouths are nevertheless put into animal bodies. The path out of our bodies is a slow one. Lacto-ovo-vegetarianism, lacto-vegetarianism, and ovo-vegetarianism are steps in the right direction, and are good compromises for and concessions to those who care not to aspire higher. This is intended only to qualify "lactism" and "ovism," not to mock them, though the rationale that some vegetarians hold against veganism sometimes sounds as pig-headed as those of carnivores'. Literal statements about calf rennet in hard cheese, bone and urine in toothpaste, lard in peanut butter and pie crust, gelatin in candy, and flesh fat in soap are often responded to with disbelief.

Metaphors about veal floating invisibly in milk and about hearts beating silently in eggs are met with blank stares. Yet veganism can no more be expected of vegetarians than vegetarianism of carnivores: all that is expected is that we know the facts.

Once the facts are learned we can gather their debris into two heaps: the ethic in the mind as theories, the dietetic in the stomach as recipes. More people are qualified speakers on nutrition than on philosophy since nutrition offers more answers with far less questioning. Furthermore, philosophy is of little value to the lamebrain dying of malnutrition. Little wonder that books on vegetable and vegetarian cooking outnumber those on vegetarianism twenty to one, and that those on vegetarianism offer more seasoning than reasoning. (You are what you eat, but you read what you are.) And once the facts are learned, then what; or rather, so what? They can be ignored or heeded: if heeded, they can be affirmed or denied; if affirmed, they can be used rightly or wrongly.

More good people than bad are alive but fewer right beliefs than wrong are shared by them: only one shortest distance between two points exists, while infinite others surround it. The world pool is polluted as much by drowning foolers as by drowned fools. If a wrong belief is based on misguidance—of false advice from sugar scientists and poison-ivy-league professors funded by blood money—on misinformation—about the myth that veal is white because the calf was milk-fed—or on misery—as of consumers and producers who know not how to differentiate sense from cents—then the believer has every grace for remaining good. Despite the daily slaughter of the innocents, the guilty and apathetic live on, blessed.

Carnivorism in no way negates goodness; it only does not let us forget evil. Some places remind us of evil more than others. In Israel, employment of teenagers is forbidden anywhere that an undesirable effect might impair their physical, emotional, or moral development. Although the army somehow fails to appear on their list, included among these forbidden places are bars, mines, mental institutions . . . and slaughterhouses. Kibbutzim may be small societies nearest to our conception of Utopia, but as long as most of them continue to tend to their chicken coops they will remain a long way from approximating Eden. Only in Eden was there no sin and, therefore, no death and, therefore, no killing and, therefore, no flesh. The "therefores" can easily be reversed. Dining tables in houses compare to and prepare for the dying tables of the operating rooms and death wards in hospitals.

Yet, despite the little we might cause others to die, we will still be eaten. Even confused Prince Hamlet understood that we fatten fish with worms, and ourselves with fish, that we ourselves might fatten worms.

The Threefold Godhead of Hinduism—Shiva, Vishnu, and Brahma—forms the door which slams shut our small square cell called life. The individual, even in sackcloth and barefoot, allows now one head to raise itself atop the body, and now another, but always the other two remain waiting. Destruction conceives the foundation of creation: we are not green, do not contain chlorophyll, cannot produce our own food, and so destroy plants. The closest we can come to complete harmlessness is fruitarianism (not necessarily "fruit-fruitarianism"), whereby the plant remains alive though we eat its produce. Though we may chop down trees for paper on which to write instructions on how not to chop down trees, at least we destroy far less than any carnivore. And our point here is that we destroy still less if we do not drink milk.

Like the active member of the Friends of Animals and the devoted worker at the ASPCA who meet each other for lunch over a steak, the vegetarian who drinks milk waits according to an obsolete timetable for the same train of thought which stops at, but goes no farther than, being a humanitarian who eats flesh. Is veganism justified? The question is answered best by the very uneasiness of the lacto-ovo-vegetarian. Is it practical? Can it be practical, can it be practiced in modern Western society? Truth owes no homage to any society, East or West, nor to any diet, worst or best. Where there is a will, there need be no whey.

One vegetarian prepared for a six-week cross-country excursion by reverting to carnivorism, though temporarily; one vegan prepared for a European six-month vagabondage by reverting to lacto-vegetarianism. The paradox is obvious, and that the former slept in first-class hotels while the latter slept in a sleeping bag is not really relevant. Realizing this, the vegetarian on a second trip continued with vegetarianism. Also realizing it, the vegan on a second trip, longer still and farther away, continued with veganism. (Truth be told, the vegan also wished not to struggle through days of vomit and weeks of diarrhea caused by indigestion until the body began again its infantile production of lactase.) Liquids assume the shape of their containers; solids do not. We finish certain books and though never referring to them again we store them on a shelf. That is important; rather than discard them we store them on a shelf. Other books we read and finish, and find so worthwhile that we begin them again. Concerning the grosser pleasures of life—smoking, drinking, doping, gambling, carousing, and flesh eating—many come to an end of these books and yet begin again; others find an end which demands no repetition, and cast them aside.

This chronology of dissimulation stresses that each be cast aside one by one in its own due time, not massively in meaningless ceremony, and be renounced not out of sacrifice but out of boredom. Indeed, the ascetic, as Tolstoy said, is one who derives more reward renouncing a small pleasure than indulging in it. We need not be sorry to have pursued and perused these volumes: quite the contrary, we can be glad to have opened them, and just as glad to have shut them closed. Though they are not worth rereading, we might store them for future reference in which to research a passage, or to quote from, devoting careful attention to acknowledging our sources. What was the text becomes the epigraph and index.

It amounts to this: development is a product not of renunciation; rather, renunciation is a product of development. An object falling to the earth constantly gains velocity only to a point, after which it moves at a steady speed. As great as may be the weight that any book contributes to the evidence, the cause of vegetarianism cannot prod carnivores who are already proceeding along life's way at their greatest pace possible, and likewise for veganism in relation to lacto-vegetarians.

"Why are you writing?" the reader asks; "Why are you reading?" the writer answers. No book should be taken on its word, and in nutrition we should evaluate the premises by the results: the readers. A book might not be told by its cover, but the body can be by its complexion. We might match reader to book; yet we can forget the book, assuming not all readers are doers, and match the people by the food they eat. It is worth seeing—though maybe not worth going to see—that the person who eats "blunder bread" and "shot dogs" looks different from one who subsists primarily on fruits and vegetables. The body overcomes food by becoming it, and overcomes bad food by becoming bad.

Milk, for instance, is natural for humans only if it is human milk and if its drinkers are less than adults. Flesh also is natural, if its eaters are willing to be less than human. And vegans who resort to B12 pills have every right to do so, if its swallowers are willing to be less than natural. For if we do not have faith in food in its natural state, then we do not have faith in (if we are believers) God or (if we are not) Nature.

So much for talk about food; let us eat it, and be done with it. All these long pages have been an invitation for dinner. You have arrived at the agreed time, and have sat down. The table is set: wooden bowls, chopsticks, cloth napkins, earthenware mugs, and candlelight. Everything appears to be ready. What is that you ask? You want to know, where is the food? What do you mean? No one told you that you were supposed to bring it? Well, good! As long as you are here, we can talk. And not about the food. For the time has come to turn to the more serious side of our subject, to matters of life and death. But we are not obligated to turn to it too seriously. After all, life is a joke, and death its laughter.

II. Ethic

It is not surprising that the lambs should bear a grudge against the great birds of prey, but that is no reason for blaming the great birds of prey for taking the little lambs. And when the lambs say among themselves, "Those birds of prey are evil, and he who is as far removed from being a bird of prey, who is rather its opposite, a lamb—is he not good?" Then there is nothing to cavil at in the setting up of this ideal, though it may also be that the birds of prey will regard it a little sneeringly, and perhaps say to themselves, "*We* bear no grudge against them, these good lambs, we even like them: nothing is tastier than a tender lamb."

> FRIEDRICH NIETZSCHE,
> *The Genealogy of Morals,*
> "Good and Evil," "Good and Bad"

6. Animals and Infidels

Because Christian morality leaves animals out of account, they are at once outlawed in philosophical morals; they are mere "things," mere means to any ends whatsoever. They can therefore be used for vivisection, hunting, coursing, bullfights, and horse racing, and can be whipped to death as they struggle along with heavy carts of stone. Shame on such a morality that is worthy of pariahs, and that fails to recognize the eternal essence that exists in every living thing, and shines forth with inscrutable significance from all eyes that see the sun!

ARTHUR SCHOPENHAUER,
On the Basis of Morality

The pages of history are written in blood, but at least the East's blood has been mostly human. The ideologies of holy books rarely correspond with the realities of history books; the religions of both East and West preach love for humans, neither region practicing what is preached. The East has much more frequently preached love for animals also and has treated them accordingly better than has the West. And yet, and yet . . . whoever compares one culture with another had better know everything about both, but who knows everything? Of all nations, India is most often cited for its concern for the cow above all animals. But it is in part a self-concern which has not much to do with animals; it is like the subdued ruthlessness of certain anti-vivisectionists who wish to abolish animal experiments only because the results rarely prove applicable to humans and when indeed applied actually prove quite disastrous. In this way, as cake in the West, India knows it cannot both eat its cows and milk them.

Just as the tractor is dear to the farmer and the family car to the father, the ox is holy to the Indian farmer and father, and the cow sacred to all because she produces both oxen and milk. Hindus react in a half-facetious manner to Western suggestions of slaughtering the cows for flesh food, but the facetiousness is underlaid with grim premonitions: the farmer would eventually have no tractor, the father no car, and the mother neither fuel from their dung nor milk for her young. In the final evaluation—since the

75

fuel is used mostly for cooking and the milk not just for weaning —the suggestions may be only half foolish, but not for the reasons Westerners intend and only so long as alternatives exist. Alas, choice is a consequence of affluence; presently India has not much choice. If most of that nation were carnivores it could not support even half of its already starving population; if everyone were free from their religion for just one year to turn the sacred cow into roast beef, the cow would become scarce and roasts would become rare. Indians would be like the Siriono, a tribe in Eastern Bolivia, who have destroyed most of their native fruit trees with their newly acquired iron tools because cutting the trees down is less an effort than climbing them.

The cow is not held so sacred as we from far away might think. A Hindu will not kill one outright but will tie an old or ill animal to a stake until she starves to death, will not slaughter a calf which competes for milk but will yoke it in such a way that its mother will not nurture it, and will not sell an ox to the butcher but will sell it to a Muslim or a Christian who will sell it to the butcher. Even within the bounds and bonds of Hinduism the Hindu gets away with murder.

In Buddhism all life is sacred though it exists in higher and lower forms. In Jainism all life is sacred and equal: there are no higher or lower forms. In Judaism and its two ungrateful children, Christianity and Islam, there are again higher and lower forms but only the highest are sacred: the members of that tradition. These two latter religions of preference and prejudice have brandished their swords wherever they have brought their gospels, and have bled the necks of those who would not bend their knees. Their goals obviously self-serving, it is no coincidence that at the dinner table almost everything else is served: consumption of a calf and a lamb is a way of converting them into Christians and Muslims.

Western religion, and to some smaller degree Western philosophy, exclude animals from their ethics as intently as flesh cookbooks leave out telling about the screams of pain and the streams of blood which came from the steak that sizzles on the grill. While philosophers construct systems of universal conduct forgetting the fifth day of creation, priests deliver sermons completely negating that day. From the very beginning the Bible gives mankind dominion (domination) over all living, moving things. To what purpose? Despite mother love and other love; despite our love for our dogs who wake us from sleep to take them for walks, and our support for the ASPCA where we put to sleep our dogs whom we have tired walking; despite humanitarians gone to Sierra Leone to medicate the poor, and gurus come to Beverly Hills to meditate the rich; despite the murals of the Sistine Chapel, and the morals of the chapel Sisters: despite the walls built by Chinese to keep out invaders, and the cathedrals built by Christians to take in the infidels; despite spaceships and satellites, and microscopes and isotopes; despite Mass, Communion, and mass communication; despite irrigation, desegregation, and group-plan hospitalization; despite all sacred scriptures and all world wisdom—we still kill other humans in the name of foolish wars, animals in the name of faddish foods, and ourselves in the name of fame and fortune. All this to what purpose? That we, created on the sixth day, might bring the entire planet to rest on the seventh, that with either a bomb or a whimper the cycle might start again if not from the very beginning then from the roaches and the rats who survive everything.

Not much oxygen or ink need be wasted denigrating Western religion; it is dead, killed by a newer creed, science, which we now must contend with, along with its most frequently performed, most obdurately wrong rite, vivisection. In the inhumane name of human progress, scientists torture animals instead of heretics, sacrificing lives for solutions instead of salvations. The over one hundred million yearly tolled tortures have proved only that animals feel pain and that scientists feel no pity.

Where religion brought hate and called it the search for divine love, science brings death and calls it the quest for eternal life.

The abolitionist battle may not be won in our lifetimes, so what we can do is use no drugs for our fetishes or cosmetics for our blemishes, nor have dealings with industries and foundations which finance researchers to throw acids and dyes into the asses and eyes of a thousand rabbits to prove again and again that the rabbits will go crazy and blind and that the scientists already are; and to force beagles to inhale smoke to ascertain which brand of cigarette least causes cancer. Is it not peculiar that both the tobacco industries and the cancer societies conduct the same experiments, seeking and getting different results? This much we can count on: when two cavalries opposed each other on the battlefield, those who always lost were the horses.

The enigma "What is life?" will never be answered in the riddled body of a vivisected animal, and may never be answered at all. Those questions which are reasonable to consider are "What is human life?" and "What is human truth?" The reason for human existence on earth will have to be sought in humans, indeed in ourselves. Christianity particularly negates individual will, and in its stead bases awareness of truth on divinity: a particular revelation in a particular place at a particular time. Plato's Idealism propounds that no revelation can bring to any individual a truth not realizable through independent speculative thought: all already possess the truth but need to be made conscious of it. Thus Christ is said to be the Truth, while Socrates' task was neither to be the truth nor to teach the truth but to awaken it from dormancy in every soul.

This difference is found between Western philosophy and Western religion, between waking from sleep and being born again out of death. Since the former is a metaphor for the latter, these are metaphysical identicals. So do we or do we not possess the truth? If we, indeed, possess it, we possessed it from the eternal beginning and shall possess it until the eternal return, and only await someone to awaken it. But if we do not possess it, then this very moment we are stupidly demonstrating to each other our separate silly untruths while awaiting messages from the Messiah. These past two millennia of patient procrastination have, however, produced no Messiah, but only a Church which selfishly served as both country and creed in treating individual will with inquisitions and crusades.

As for its treatment of animals, Pope Innocent VIII of the Renaissance required that when witches were burned, their cats be burned with them; Pope Pius IX of a century ago forbade the formation of an SPCA in Rome, declaring humans had no duty to animals; Pope Pius XII of World War II stated that when animals are killed in slaughterhouses or laboratories, " . . . their cries should not arouse unreasonable compassion any more than do red-hot metals undergoing the blows of the hammer;" and Pope Paul VI in 1972, when blessing a batallion of Spanish bullfighters, became the first Pope to bestow his benediction upon the one cruelty which even the Church had condemned. The fights have always been held on Catholic feast days; in fact, one of the stylized sweeps of the toreador's cape is called the Veronica, as though used to wipe the tears of the bull on his way to crucifixion.

The implications for discussion of diet are these: the Pre-Socratic, Socratic and Platonic, and Neo-Platonic philosophers were generally vegetarians, whereas Rabbis bless butcher knives and Rembrandt's paintings of slaughtered oxen hardly differ from his depictions of crucified Christs, despite Christ's own command to replace flesh with bread and blood with wine. Weighing the solipsism of Idealism against the serendipity of Christianity, we must seek advice of philosophers and forget the priests. Yet philosophers, also human, share in making mistakes. Even gods err: that Jews, Christians, and Muslims cite passages in their holy books which defend carnivorism and animal exploitation means either that theirs are wrong books or wrong gods.

We by no means wish to write the history of philosophy or religion any more than of vegetarianism or carnivorism. Just as the philosophy of history is more interesting than the history of philosophy, any new philosophy of vegetarianism is more important than any history of vegetarianism or even history of the philosophy of vegetarianism: the truly new inherently incorporates the old. Animals have found many friends in philosophers, several of whom are creditors for the epigraphic seeds scattered throughout these leaves. Nevertheless, a handful of venom-mouthed zoophobes have bookwormishly wiggled their way within the pages of the history of philosophy. The most notorious of these is Descartes, who was not only a vivisectionist but also a vivisector, not only a calculating mathematician but also a Catholic theologian. Like a judge condemning a criminal whose one offense was having been born a non-human, Descartes' single sentence has incited more persecution of animals than any one utterance of Hitler or Stalin concerning the prisoners of their death camps. Pointing to a dissected calf, he said that there he found his library—and he tortured and burned his sources.

Cogito ergo sum. "I think, therefore I am." Assuming animals could not speak, he doubted they could think. Assuming they could not think, he doubted they could feel. Assuming they could not feel, he doubted their very existence. According to Descartes, animals behaved without the intervention of a soul, hence without consciousness, and were mere machines, animal-automatons made of wheels and weights like clocks. This originated in his study of the pineal gland, which he believed was moved by the soul to affect the mind. Never finding the pineal gland through his sad scratchings inside the skulls of his victims, he altogether disregarded their brains. Although subsequent animal maulers indeed located the gland, no one has yet found any wheels or weights. Such are the results of labors in the laboratory "library."

Descartes was on one of the many not quite parallel tracks of truth when he separated mind from matter, but came to a halt when designating animals as all matter, and deviated completely when claiming that animals did not matter. Philosophy's pendulum swings in one direction in one generation, the opposite direction in the next generation, and sometimes dizzily in all directions at once. Like science, but unlike religion, it does not hesitate to refute in the morning everything it had vowed the night before. It is weakness to take credit when one is right, but strength to admit when one is wrong. Thus philosophy is democratic: it esteems its Descartes but also its Montaigne, whose "Apology for Raimond Sebond" posits animal instincts as surpassing our intelligence, and their stupidity our wisdom. Furthermore, philosophy forms not just a democracy but also a plurality: to this day Cartesians claim to know exactly what an animal is, but then they think they know what everything is.

History—that great funnel at which the sands of science, religion, and philosophy all converge as they measure our time—rallies behind terse maxims, for they must be short else easily forgotten. Even "I think, therefore I am," is the truncation for "I doubt, therefore I think therefore I am," which could be the battle cry of mankind's soldiers in its war against the animal kingdoms. ("I kill, therefore I am" would be closer to the call.) As the slaughterer slits the throat of every chicken which passes on the disassembly line, he may whisper, "I think therefore I am; I think therefore I am; I think therefore I am." The obverse, "I do not think therefore I am not," he must imagine to be echoed by every chicken, or anyway by the rasping of his dull blade severing its neck.

Cartesian logic was one of philosophy's greatest stumblings, comparable in kind but not degree to religion's greatest of all stumblings, the Church. From philosophy's worst zoological blunder we shall leap back two thousand years to its first blunder. Terse maxims are often intended by their makers to mean something completely opposite to that which history interprets. Greatness indeed is commensurable with being misunderstood: the greater the space allocated in eternity's ledger, the more one is likely to be misunderstood. The possibility must not be overlooked that we completely misinterpret Descartes. But no doubt exists that another such misconstrued thinker is Protagoras and his decree, "Man is the measure of all things."

History, that is, human history, would have us believe this to mean that all is measured with humanity as its standard, that we are everything, that the whole of the universe in our absence amounts to nothing. This fits right into schemes for subjugation of the planet, the plants, and of course the animals, from the oxen who must bear their yokes to the chickens who must bare their necks. Yet we people and all the finned, feathered, and furred are common vassals sharing the same single crust of earth, beggars scrounging for the same single crust of bread.

Actually, the Greek translation is not "Man is" but "*A* man is the measure of all things." The additional article is crucial. The former signifies "humanity" while the latter "a human." In Plato's *Theaetetus* (161c), Socrates says, "I am surprised that he [Protagoras] did not begin his *Truth* with the words, the measure of all things is the pig, or the baboon, or some sentient creature still more uncouth." Perception, not erudition, is the root of all conception. Those who see, know. Socrates further says that if animals also perceive they also are measures, if the tadpole is an animal then the tadpole is the measure of all things, and then what it judges for itself is as proper as what any human judges.

If what every human judges is right and true, if each is the measure of individual wisdom " . . . then where is our comparative ignorance or the need for us to go and sit at his [Protagoras'] feet?" Those with clear vision could as well sit at the feet of a pig, a baboon, or a rabbit, as of Protagoras, Descartes, or even Socrates. Bu for those without such sight, hardly enough feet can be found. This could be the origin of carrying a rabbit's foot as a good luck charm.

Imagine walking along a forest trail, suddenly you stop; you hear a sound and spot a rabbit crouched motionlessly, she having spotted you. The two actions are similar, only the intentions differ: you had stopped in order to see, she had stopped in order not to be seen. As she stops and stares at you, you stand and stare at her; so long as you do not move, she does not move . . . and you two still might be standing and staring. She hides from you because she had no evidence whether you were harmless or not. A child out to kill time, in no hurry to grow up, might have thrown a stone at her; or a hunter simply out to kill, who has never grown up, might have shot her. The rabbit hides out of habit because of the bad reputation caused by the stones and guns of crazed carnivores.

Such a conclusion as the above will no doubt appear to the flesh eater a product of specious logic that only the vegetarian or humanitarian is capable of. Carnivores could protest that they are not so cruel as to kill rabbits. They also might have felt a hesitant sense of offense by "Warning: I Brake for Animals" bumper stickers, once so popularly displayed, whose fluorescent inference was that those not bearing such an emblem should be suspected of driving callously and on the warpath. But brake as they might on the road, how many of these alert drivers gave a break to animals at the dinner table?

Just as it is contradictory for the humanitarian not to be a vegetarian, so it is for the carnivore not to stone rabbits. Anyone strolling in the woods and happening upon a patch of ripe red raspberries might not conceive of picking them because of fullness of stomach, laziness of body, hesitancy of mind at trying things new, or preference to leave the berries to the rabbits. Likewise the carnivore might not try to stone the rabbit because of fullness, or laziness, or hesitancy at trying something not wrapped in pre-priced cellophane, or preference to leave the rabbit to the hawks. Only through self-deception can a carnivore claim the wish to leave the rabbit to itself, and thereby disclaim cruelty, for if someone else were to stone it, a second person to skin it, a third to cook it, and a fourth to serve it, it is clear who would be the fifth and sixth to pay for and to eat it. "We have rabbits" reads the sign outside a store, which at first glance appears to be a pet shop but is actually the butcher.

Strato the Peripatetic observed that without intelligence animals cannot perceive. When Dr. Kellogg of the cornflake asked, "How can you eat anything that has eyes?" he was also asking how anyone with intelligence can eat anything that is also ruled by intelligence. It is one thing to eat intelligently, another thing to dine on intelligence itself. An animal that has eyes (or that once had them, as in the case of cavefish, or that maintain the organ but not its operation, as in the case of the blind) has a brain to convert visual perceptions into logical conceptions. Do not even the smallest of animals with even the smallest of brains also think, though these be even the smallest of thoughts? The pea-sized cerebrums of dinosaurs may or may not have been contributing factors to their extinction, but their dominion on the earth was nevertheless far longer than ours has been. These thoughts of nature, though not always the nature of these thoughts, are as evident as the eyes before our own. Who are so blind they cannot see that the rabbit also sees, and who so dull not to think the rabbit also thinks? It stares at you out of rabbit eyes just as you stare at it out of human eyes, and thinks of you through a rabbit mind just as you think of it through a human mind. The hawk too sees the rabbit out of hungry hawk eyes, and so on . . . for the hawk should no more eat berries than a rabbit eat hawks. We do not expect a child to think like an adult. So why expect an animal to think like a human?

All humans think differently from one another, and animals think differently from each other and from humans. This is not disparity, but diversity. Each new thinker is merely a new scale by which to measure the world. Armchair travelers with rules in hand measure nothing: we must stand up, stretch out our arms, and set the rules against the objects. A man is not the measure of *all* things, but only of things which can be reached. And a collection of centimeters is not always a ruler, but only if arranged in a straight line. Yet even a straight ruler well within reach of what is to be measured is no evidence of proper use. Speech has been the mark of thought in a world where words alone offer meager proofs. The childish, the tongue-tied, the hare-brained, and the bird-brained are all the same pejoratives.

Hardly enough to be just humans, we who stand up and are counted must be thinking humans. While we are omnivores all, while some are largely carnivores, while many more are wholly herbivores, while the rest of our species moderates according to necessity—which in the world other than the West leaves few options other than vegetarianism—ours is still the singular species of choice. Not all of us exercise that choice: most remain at rest in the vestibule of indecision by letting either waiters or mothers, (or, in the case of some males, their other mothers, their wives) choose the dinner. Socrates says to "Know Oneself" and Kierkegaard to "Choose Oneself." Vegetarians, through thought and action, choose themselves, while the rest of the West lose themselves: the sons and the husbands by not choosing, the mothers and wives by choosing nothing new.

We do not choose between birth and death; birth and death choose us. We do choose between life and suicide. Is life worth living? Assuming the affirmative, without further questions, our second query is how we should live, and our third is who should live. Mix together these ingredients of inquiry into a recipeless stone soup, cook the soup for four hours over the heated arguments concerning what food is worth eating, and in time for dinner—though it will then be served cold—we will have prepared one big question to chew on: "What life is worth eating?"

After separating the sheep from the goats and sifting the wheat from the chaff, next we must elect whether to keep the sheep from the wheat or to mix them into the soup. This, of course, is the choice of vegetarianism, of carnivorism, or of neither; of hesitation and negation, the supreme existential condition: starvation. These developments of conscience and consciousness few initiate and fewer conclude. That we are alive is no testament to an affirmation of life any more than is flesh eating testament to any negation; not killing ourselves on the one hand, and killing animals on the other, are owed neither to consent nor denial but to ossification and superficiality. In any case the opposite of the suicide is the vegetarian, and the large numbers of each suggest a lot of people have been doing a lot of thinking.

Many people think that only people think. They have stared too long at their mirrors without mentally stepping aside to glimpse the animal within the human they reflect upon. How can they justify killing animals unless their thesis supports killing humans? Can such support truly exist? Dostoyevsky's Kirilov, in *The Possessed*, perhaps came close in his arguments, but only for killing himself. In his mind, the suicide exalts himself into a god, into a being whose actions beckon beyond others' commands. Lucky for other humans and animals, Kirilov, once a god, could take no further life. Animals, like gods, need not rationalize their actions either. So that they can get away with what they cannot explain away, humans who kill animals can equate themselves only with animals. The commandment "Thou Shalt Not Kill" may or may not have been spoken about animals. It certainly was not spoken to animals. And it certainly was not spoken by a prophet who practiced what he preached. The brain is like a gland which secretes thoughts. Carnivores who eat flesh saturated with animal hormones will think animal thoughts. Rabbit-eaters will become either more like rabbits or less like rabbits and more like hawks that also eat rabbits. But rabbit or hawk, they become less human. Berries secrete no such thoughts; berry-eating rabbits remain rabbits just as berry-eating humans remain humans. Under these circumstances animals gain every advantage in eating humans, but humans absolutely none in eating animals. Under these circumstances the only animals humans should risk eating are other humans. Under these circumstances the human with better-than-average intelligence runs greater risks than does someone whose intellect is less than average.

That the brain is a gland which secretes thoughts is a thought first attributed to an old philosopher whom we did not have to eat to know this, but had only to read. Whether we eat him or read him, we do not have to believe him. Some people believe everything they read, some only what they read. Some will believe only what they see, or if blind, then only what they hear. Perhaps people believe animals do not think because no animal has told them otherwise. Human infants not yet cognizant of human language are certainly not denied the capability of learning it, of speaking through it, eventually of thinking through it. And dare anyone point to a mute's inability to speak as evidence of incapacity to think? Animals cannot learn human speech because they do not have human mouths, not just because they do not have human brains. Not until the 1950s was it finally recognized that apes' vocal tracts are incapable of human speech. Wonders of science . . . and of vivisection!

Many methods of communication exist. Speech and sound are not singular. Some animals depend more on sight, others on smell, many on touch. Some fishes signal electrically; fireflies flash lights; honeybees dance. Certain animals incapable of human speech can nevertheless learn human symbols. This has been demonstrated over and over again in research with chimpanzees who have mastered hundreds of words in American Sign Language. Their statements are at times pure poetry. Washoe, the first of these, coined the phrases ''rock berry'' for the Brazil nut and ''apple which is orange'' for the orange. Lucy, another ape poet of the post-beaten generation, called the hot radish ''cry hurt food'' and the watermelon ''drink fruit.'' And the caged Washoe once signaled to a sympathetic visitor, ''Get me out of here!''

As is now known to be true for porpoises, dolphins, and whales, animals converse extensively in their own vocabularies. Some even sing. As philologians we must blame only ourselves for so long neglecting to learn their languages. We say in English that we need only learn French or German or Italian to love the people and cultures of France or Germany or Italy. Those who are more interested in paté au foie gras, liverwurst and salami should strive to learn the more universal screams of pain of the slaughterhouse.

Some will still deny animals their thoughts just to deny them their lives: the life of thought must encompass the thought of life. Until such denials cease, no rapprochement will materialize, for the concordance must be in terms not of animals' inability to speak our many languages, of which most of us can speak but one, but of ours to hear and understand theirs. (If we are so smart, why have we taken so long?) The lack of understanding is attributable as much to our ears which refuse to hear their languages as their tongues which refuse to speak ours.

Dogs hear pitches beyond our range; dolphins both hear and emit such sounds. Dolphins understand each other and to a considerable extent understand us; some even understand we cannot understand them, for they have been known to keep their quacking and whistling within our auditory abilities when in our presence. That they understand when we do not understand them is a considerably greater accomplishment than our own understanding.

Meanwhile we had better watch out. Just before he turned against the world in a rage of destruction, the monster of vivisection in Mary Shelley's *Frankenstein* observed: "Sometimes I wished to express my sensations in my own mode, but the uncouth and inarticulate sounds which broke from me frightened me into silence again." If dolphins, for instance, could speak in human language, and specifically in English, perhaps the first thing they would say is "A Dolphin is the measure of all things." Yet they remain reticent.

In 1823, America introduced enforced silence in its prisons. Thus the land of liberty became the first to employ the cruelest of all punishments. Perhaps dolphins, like our silent deities, wish to punish us. Or perhaps they simply do not wish to be misunderstood. Animals, who all walk barefoot through the streets of Athens, never need to read to know themselves. The question remains whether we humans will know ourselves, for in so knowing we will surely know that we too are animals and that all animals already know themselves. Meanwhile, until animals stoop to humans' language, no words express more for the cause of vegetarianism than do "Oink!", "Moo!", and "Cock-A-Doodle-Doo!"

7. Carnivoral Death and Karmic Debt

A Robin Red Breast in a Cage
Puts all Heaven in a Rage.
A dove house fill'd with doves & pigeons
Shudders Hell thro' all its regions
A dog starv'd at his Master's Gate
Predicts the ruin of the State.
A Horse misus'd upon the Road
Calls to Heaven for Human blood.
Each outcry of the hunted Hare
A fibre from the Brain does tear.
A Skylark wounded in the wing,
A Cherubim does cease to sing.
The Game Cock clip'd & arm'd for fight
Does the Rising Sun affright.
Every Wolf's & Lion's howl
Raises from Hell a Human Soul.
The wild deer, wand'ring here & there,
Keeps the Human Soul from Care.
The Lamb misus'd breeds Public strife
And yet forgives the Butcher's knife.
The Bat that flits at close of Eve
Has left the Brain that won't Believe.
The Owl that calls upon the Night
Speaks the Unbeliever's fright.
He who shall hurt the little Wren
Shall never be belov'd by Men.
He who the Ox to wrath has mov'd
Shall never be by Woman lov'd.
The wanton Boy that kills the Fly
Shall feel the Spider's enmity.
He who torments the Chafer's sprite
Weaves a Bower in endless Night.
The Catterpiller on the Leaf
Repeats to thee thy Mother's grief.
Kill not the Moth nor Butterfly,
For the Last Judgement draweth nigh.
He who shall train the Horse to War
Shall never pass the Polar Bar.
The Beggar's Dog & Widow's Cat,
Feed them & thou wilt grow fat.

from WILLIAM BLAKE'S
"Auguries of Innocence"

87

It is very interesting to consider the lilies of the field, and also very easy; let us instead try considering the wool moths in our wardrobe closets and the cockroaches in our kitchen cabinets. If we kept our cupboards clean the cockroaches would bother us less. But the one food above others upon which they thrive is grease, the cooking of which causes splattering more than any other food. It is entirely fitting that the fat of animals which many people like most to eat should attract the feet of other little animals which most people like least to see. Likewise for the moths in our bedrooms: it is absolutely appropriate that the one species of animal that eats our sweaters eats only an article of clothing made from another species of animal.

We could resort to boric acid and camphor, in which case it is entirely fitting and absolutely appropriate that what is meant in a big way to poison little animals such as cockroaches and moths, will also in a little way, poison big animals such as ourselves. We pay more to kill them than to let them survive, for such is the mentality of our nuclear age. Civil wars are viewed as conflicts which have no winners but, whether civil war or world war, both sides always lose. We already know that in the next world war there will be neither winners nor losers; there will be no one.

An Irishman might feel solidarity with other Irishmen, or a Catholic with other Catholics, or an Englishman with other Englishmen, or a Protestant with other Protestants. Those who feel less distinction between themselves and others if white might feel solidarity with other whites, or if male with other males. The truly noble mind discerns no differences and feels affinity with all humanity. Yet this too is limited. Why stop at humans? Should we not reach to the whole of life? And why stop at life? Albert Schweitzer's own reverance for life reached beyond the leaf that he dared not pluck to the icicle that he dared not shatter. The less unique we think ourselves, the more we feel ourselves in all that surrounds us and the more we feel what surrounds us in ourselves.

Surrendering to surrounding, we should understand that two things moving along similar paths probably began from similar origins: we should realize our common bond with animals, all animals, not just the butterflies but also the moths. To fail to do so, and to fail to teach our children to do so, will cause our children to fail to recognize their common bond with us. Those who see no further than their own egos and the egos' barricades, their bodies, imitate Thyestes, burying their teeth in their own flesh because they delude themselves that it is the flesh of another animal. Our knowledge of our origin places us above animals, yet the fact that that origin is out of animals only draws us back down again. Humans should acknowledge their debt to the animal kingdom; but rather than pay them back humans eat them up.

A large part of the human world—the part which eats few or no animals—believes in the concept of transmigration of souls, which instructs that people who kill animals will be reborn as animals to suffer the same death. But time, reaching into infinity and disregarding continuity, knows no waiting: humans destined to return as those animals are at once the animals killed and the humans killing them. "This thou art; all is one." We are all one; but, like two close friends at a restaurant, we are billed separately. We who break free from the bondage of our own passions recognize ourselves in the objects of our passions, recognize ourselves as objects of others' passions, and finally recognize ourselves and others as the passion itself. We who break from the bondage of passion demonstrate our freedom in one way: compassion.

Karma means action. The Eastern law of karma might be defined in various Western ways: scientifically as action and reaction, epistemologically as cause and effect, biblically and botanically as sowing and reaping, and even economically as supply and demand. This law is mitigated not by the temporal justice of a temporal state, but by the eternal justice of the stars. No angel sits in Heaven calculating crimes soon to be punished when the offenders approach their personal nemeses; rather, punishments are begun the moment crimes are committed. We need believe neither in the omnipresence of the biblical God nor in the *pasas* of the Vedic Varuna to see that the killing of an animal in even the darkest corner of the deepest cave does not escape notice: the animal sees by the same dim light as does its killer.

Killer and killed, tormentor and tormented, eater and eaten, sheep and shepherd and slaughterer, are one. The one who runs after is no less compelled than the one who runs away. The dog chasing the rabbit is no different than the dog chasing its tail. During pursuit the predator is as much its own victim as is its prey. Victim suffers by being eaten, assailant by simply being. Nature is undeniably cruel and life unmentionably cheap, but one way we can rise above life is by not taking it.

We wander from one life to the next, and meanings meander from one word to another: metempsychosis, palingenesis, transmigration, and reincarnation all essentially mean the same but do not look the same, nor did they become words at the same time. Whether we know or believe their meanings, we need investigate neither from the next life nor into the past life to discern that the most unfortunate of all are those who cause misfortune to others. Maybe as many teeth are broken on bones in fish as on pebbles in lentils, but certainly more fishers are lost at sea than are irrigators to alligators. Maybe as many hunters as harvestors are struck by lightning, but certainly more hunters die of gunshot than do harvestors of sunstroke. Maybe as many butchers' fingers as lumberjacks' are hacked by their own axes, but certainly butchers contract more sickness and boils from the blood on their hands than do lumberjacks from the sap and the soil on their lands. And when people choke to death on what they eat, what makes them meet their end most often is an end of meat.

While eating fruit is the reverse of eating flesh, the inverse of eating animals is being eaten by animals. Two thousand years, counted backwards or forwards, matter little to our particular present moment in history: once Christians were thrown to the lions, now lambs are thrown to Christians. Humans with lamb chops in their choppers will have to wait forever for the day "The wolf shall dwell with the lamb, and the leopard shall lie down with the kid . . . and the lion shall eat straw like the ox" (Isaiah 11:6,7). The angry prophet somehow failed to mention that humans too must sit in peace with the lamb, the kid, and the ox on the holy mountain, not just on the table top.

Can a wrong "here" be rectified by a right "there"? There would be no wolves, leopards, or lions in the wild if there were no deer, gazelles, or zebras; nor would there be any lambs, kids, or oxen on the farm if there were no farmers. But if there were no farmers or farms, there would be lots of wilderness and wild animals. Nevertheless, some will still try to defend the slaughterhouse by suggesting that the farm animals would not otherwise have entered the world except for human-controlled breeding. Such lecher logic of Stoic reductionism can be typical only of those whose chief concerns are that they themselves remain well fed—upon well-fed animals. This is not humanitarianism but premeditated murder.

While many will defend flesh as a proper food, who will defend murder as a proper deed? Proper food is necessary for a healthy body and brain, and proper thoughts are needed for what dwell within them. Who will defend murder as a proper thought? If our killing a cat which was about to kill a bird could be justified with

CARNIVORAL DEATH AND KARMIC DEBT   91

the thought that our action saved the life of the bird, then we could justify the cat's killing the bird which was about to kill a fly—whereby we could no longer justify our killing the cat. The point is that no human is capable of such broad vision as to be able to determine who should live and who should die. As it is, our judgement usually depends not on what criteria we weigh, but on what we throw away. Two people see a steak: one thinks of the mushrooms that go on top of it and then eats the steak; the other thinks of the murder that goes into it and then eats only the mushrooms.

The Buddha prohibited animal slaughter but not necessarily animal eating. Thus carnivorism was to be tolerated so long as the animal died of its own accord. Though he disparaged both killing and eating flesh, the difference is not disparate enough; many Buddhists today are carnivores. But the Buddhism that developed after Buddha is no more the responsibility of Buddha than is contemporary Christianity the responsibility of Christ. Buddha and Christ are one, but Buddhism and Christianity are quite another.

In the East, the traditional eating utensils are chopsticks, pieces of wood which imitate the very vegetables they lift; in the West they are knives and forks, pieces of cold steel which rip and puncture flesh like nails of the crucifix. Christianity speaks of the unknown world of afterlife awaiting only humans, Eastern religions of this known world of rebirth awaiting all animals. The torment of eternal damnation in Hell is an inborn idea only of a religion whose society has fostered the slaughterhouse and concentration camp, and whose little children believe as equally in Santa Claus as in Satan. Little wonder Hindus view existence in this world as the worst imaginable. Our Western assumption that life is worth all its pain and sorrow is one with which Hindus and Buddhists would not agree, but their detachment from suffering does not cause undue callousness. Conversely, Western attachment certainly has not cured it.

Judeo-Christian belief in human dignity begins in Genesis, where we are told we were made in God's image, but nowhere do we read that animals were made in humans' own image. How then can we analogize ourselves as gods to animals, giving and taking as we please? To seek the root of carnivorism in the West we must seek the root of Christianity—Judaism. Moses the messenger brought down the decree "Thou shalt not kill." Period. While coveting refers specifically to a neighbor's spouse, or honoring to one's parents, prohibition against killing is not specific: it says simply and purely not to kill. The Ten Commandments were too demanding. His people could not uphold the Law, so Moses gave them a hundred less difficult ordinances: for instance, allowing them to kill animals so that they should at least not kill humans, permitting them to eat "clean" beasts but not "unclean." This contrasts with Seventh-Day Adventism, which being Christian, considers *all* animals vermin; thus half its adherents are vegetarians.

A kosher Jew is furthermore forbidden to eat an animal, even one from a "clean" family, that has died on its own accord (Deuteronomy 14:21); whereas, a Buddhist is allowed *only* such an animal. But what is really being prohibited by Judaism is to eat an animal that has lived on its own accord. A kosher Jew is also forbidden the blood of an animal (Leviticus 17:12, and elsewhere), so kosher killing today entails evangelistic evisceration of the larger blood vessels by cutthroat butchers. But no matter how much they drain, blood will remain! They can no more squeeze all blood out of a carcass than squeeze any blood out of a stone. This might be read as a message, admittedly apocryphal and certainly secret, that "kosher kill" is yet another contradiction of adjective with noun. But we do not speak about Judaism as anti-Semites, nor about Christianity as outraged Jews, but about Judaism and Christianity from the viewpoint of slaughtered animals.

Great pains are taken by housewives to keep a carnivorous home kosher, but these are nothing compared to the greater pains inflicted on animals in suffering a kosher death. American kosher kill involves this: shackling the animal by its hind legs, or leg, hoisting it above the pool of blood from the previous victim, and then with one swift stroke of a sharp knife cutting the jugular vein through which blood will flow profusely since the animal hangs upside-down. Compared with other crude and cruel means, such as bludgeoning, or dull-bladed knifing, or letting the animal thrash around on the ground while blood only hesitantly trickles out from a poorly placed gash, for thousands of years the kosher method of killing remained the most humane. But science in this century has devised still more efficient and more merciful modes, which religion, in its last death throes, refuses to recognize. Although less than five percent of the flesh in the United States is bought kosher, as much as fifty percent of the animals are slaughtered as such. Meanwhile, just as anti-vivisectionists are branded as misanthropes, we who raise our voices against the golden kosher calf are labeled anti-Semites.

Is it a coincidence that in the middle of Moses' Five Books, the Book of Leviticus, following directly after instructions of which animals to sacrifice and how to eat them, advises how to contend with leprosy and plague? But enough. Use and misuse of Biblical passages are not an honest means of proof for any argument. For every person who points to a passage in it which supports vegetarianism, another person can find a passage which justifies carnivorism. Schopenhauer does both at once: in *On the Basis of Morality* (section 7 of Chapter 9) and *Parerga and Paralipomena* (Chapter 177 of Volume II), he outlines carnivorism's origin out of that ancient book of eternal ambiguity and thereby argues against the validity, not of vegetarianism, but of the Bible. In many cases the Bible is a shining mirror that reflects the images of whoever uses it, tired of their echoes against the blank walls of philosophy.

The search for dubious reasons never truly justifies what we believe since we already were believers without those reasons and will continue in those beliefs, reasons or no. At best these reasons are erected as pretty facades to entice others to enter the houses in which we were born and in which we shall probably die. (Truth be told, such has been the case in reference to the various passages quoted from the Bible throughout these pages: they never lend support, but act only as embellishments.) Sometimes, keeping in mind the right reasons, we still persist in doing the wrong things; or we do the right things, but for the completely wrong reasons.

Then there are the wrong things done for the wrong reasons. None has the right to kill an animal, but who can even consider the right to consume it who has not killed it? Quite the opposite, people excuse their eating the animal because someone else killed it. They hardly differ from patrons of stolen merchandise who rationalize their means of acquisition by saying someone else had stolen it.

Many do kill what they eat. In Italian towns chickens with tied feet and geese with clipped wings are sold live in the market, a carnivoral carnival. One sale between two old women lasted fifteen minutes before an agreement was settled, during which the buyer clutched the chicken by the legs, several times unknowingly and uncaringly banged its head against the ground, weighed it while yanking it to and fro, and finally dumped it into her sack. Then she must have forgotten something, pulled the chicken out again, but only halfway, stuck its legs into the railings of a nearby fence, left it dangling undoubtedly with broken legs and walked away—hunch-backed and limping. Either she abused all her chickens out of spite or she only later in life walked warped as a consequence of the chickens who, once eaten, could easily return her abuse.

When a dog bites a stranger, whose fault is it? The stranger's, for intending to pet it? The dog's, for not trusting strangers? The owner's, for training the dog not to trust strangers? Or society's, for forcing owners to train dogs not to trust strangers? "Beware of Dog" signs are quite superfluous when accompanied by the bark of a dog, but the dog itself is an excessive safeguard when announced by the more congenial sign "Beware of God." Yet both our guard dogs and our gods' dogmas are powerless puppets whose paws and laws are manifestations of karmic consequence.

The Christian attitude toward the human purpose of life is punishment and atonement originating from the Fall. Individual guilt is measured by personal pain. We are made responsible for our own actions, which set in motion the causation or cessation of our suffering; thus we are made responsible for our own suffering. People who are hurt in automobiles unhesitatingly accuse the drivers of negligence at the moment of the accident, but they dare not search their own lives to perceive the destiny which required them initially to enter the car. The fault is as much in the driver as in the driven. The fault is not in the cars, but in ourselves. Likewise, people stricken with sickness quickly blame the food they ate, yet rarely blame themselves for having eaten it.

With open eyes, an unprejudiced mind, a clear conscience, and a rudimentary understanding of metaphysics, we can welcome all life's tragedies. None need sing the Vedic hymns or recite the Book of Job to perceive that a cause lurks behind every effect, and that another effect waits ahead of that first one. A moral rarely is told in one tale, but begins in one and ends in another. The following two absolutely true episodes of karmic consequence illustrate the game of life which has no losers, only beginners.

As a natural hygienist, Mary ate no flesh, fish, milk or eggs, nor did she pop vitamin pills. Her excellent health nevertheless did not ward off her worry over possible B12 deficiency about which conventional nutritionists warned. To alleviate her paranoia after many years of veganism, she brought home a wedge of raw goat milk cheese and ate a very small piece with her supper of sprouts and greens. She left the cheese on her kitchen table and went out for the evening. When she returned the cheese was still there, though little else. As though the cheese were milked from a Trojan horse, for the first time in her life her apartment had been robbed.

Ted, a strict ethical vegan, was also a photographer. For his every roll of film, Kodak or Agfa utilized a thin layer of gelatin to adhere the light-sensitive emulsion to the film. And for this gelatin, Swift or Armour pulverized a horse's hoofs or a pig's bones. Ted knew this, yet as long as no alternatives existed he had no choice. Better that he should be in the darkroom than that his audience should be in the dark.

He never expected any carnivore to become a vegetarian or to feel guilty about eating flesh. But he did expect that a carnivore who did feel guilty should become a vegetarian. Likewise, he never expected any vegetarian to become a vegan or to feel guilty about drinking milk. But he did expect that a vegetarian who did feel guilty should become a vegan. All this he acknowledged, yet he could not give up his camera despite the guilt he felt about the gelatin on the film.

One day his apartment was burglarized. Everything was ransacked but little was stolen. In fact the only missing item of any value was his camera. Ted took much convincing to renounce his suspicion that the thief was an escaped chimp from the zoo six blocks away. At least one other person believed all the apes were criminals, because someone had already locked them behind bars.

Just as zoos are animal prisons, slaughterhouses are prisoner-of-war camps in humanity's undeclared war against animals: hence the setting for Vonnegut's novel about American POW's in the German *Slaughterhouse Five*. A still closer link is forged between slaughterhouses and concentration camps, where human inmates were herded like sheep, carted like cattle, and slaughtered like animals. One concentration camp in fact was located near a slaughterhouse and sausage factory, perhaps so that the odor from the ovens of the camp might be mistaken for the stench of the slaughter or of the sausage. Upon liberation, the camp survivors who wandered off in search of food came first to the sausage factory. Despite the pleas of temperance from a vegetarian among them, some gorged themselves so fully that one died from the sausage. He survived the concentration camp, but not the sausage factory.

The American Army liberated Buchenwald on April 11, 1945. When will it free the inmates of America's own Animal Auschwitzes? Western religions long ago ceased animal slaughter at the altar, but not yet at the abattoir. Signs outside historic Roman churches remind tourists to act respectfully since we after all are entering a place of worship. But why should we conduct ourselves any differently in than out? Why not a whole world of worship? What we would never think of doing inside, we should try not doing outside. Who would kill a calf in a cathedral? On the other hand, if trees grew in churches or if services were conducted in orchards, we need never think twice about picking fruit from their branches.

Either the chick breaks from its shell from within and is born, or it waits to be cracked from without and dies in the mouth of the predator or the frying pan of a human. Although established Western religions offer no encouragement for vegetarianism, we need not go to India in search of reasons or ways. If we should decide to go . . . on the way, we will see in Spain bulls slowly speared to death, in Italy chickens being played with by children who had strength enough only to sever half their necks, in Greece kids bleeding away in the rear of butcher shops while their legs are led away in the front of the shops by customers satisfied with the freshness of the flesh, in Turkey fish scaled while still alive . . . and we have not yet crossed the bridge into Asia.

We may like to think of Hinduism as synonymous with vegetarianism; in fact, no more than three-quarters of all Hindus are vegetarians, and of the last quarter some have reverted even to animal sacrifice. This practice is so widespread in some places—Nepal, for one—that the Buddhist is easily differentiated from the Hindu by the fact that the former never conducts the carnose ceremony.

Few answers can be found in India that cannot be found in Indiana, providing we provide questions.

If answers cannot be found in ourselves, they will hardly be found at all. A mosque, temple, or church signifies neither less than the actual practices of its congregants nor more than the preachings of its scriptures. Vegetarianism may lack a concrete house of worship, but to its benefit it also lacks the slaughterhouse; and it does have its congregants who also have their books, though sometimes these are only cookbooks.

Physically, a holy place is just a pile of bricks cemented by a heap of mortar. Lay a pile of bricks one atop the other, and you have a wall; set five such walls together, one as a roof, and you have a house . . . a house of bricks. The bricks remain individually visible within the wall, and will remain visible again as a pile long after the wall collapses. Eat a dozen apples day after day and you have built another sort of house of worship, a human body . . . a body from apples, not of apples. The apples disappear right inside of your very eyes, never again to be seen. The body does not become apples; the apples become body. Just as conquerors in an occupied land naturalize the population by forced conversion to a new religion, forced learning of a new language, and even forced feeding of a new food, so does the body overcome food by forcing food to become body. Given the choice of battling a lion, a lark, or a leek, least harm comes to everyone by waging war against the leek. External conflicts fought with tooth and nail parallel those internal fought with tooth and intestine. Cannibals ate only their enemies.

As in ambush by an army, the moment food enters the mouth it is surrounded by the body in its struggle to sustain itself in the face of foreigners. Similarly, from the day a new pair of shoes is worn, the feet form blisters to protect the skin against the untamed skin of another animal until the leather at last attains the shape of the foot; this is called "breaking in." The struggle between what is shoes is the same as between what is chewed; if an allergic reaction develops, this is called "breaking out." Like a rocket shot straight up into the air which, before plummeting, for a suspended second stands perfectly still, eater and eaten momentarily become one. Once ingested and until digested, food is a foreign material; the more complex the food, the greater difficulty the body has in digesting it. We already know that an animal is more complex than a plant, that flesh takes four hours to be digested but fruit only one. Physically, a kilogram of flesh equals a kilogram of apples, but digestively flesh lays far heavier on the stomach since like magic—abracadaver!—it was transformed from ten kilograms of apples.

Since flesh food is plant food already transformed into an animal, might not one animal body prove most suitable as food for another animal body? The proposition would be correct if animal digestion were a process of simple assimilation. Rather, food is broken down until the source is no longer recognizable; then the simple substance is rebuilt into a different but complex material, namely the animal body. Plant food, resisting the animal eater least, is thus more readily transformed. The body which consumes flesh produces much mucus as protection from digesting itself in trying to digest something which is nearly the same as itself. No people literally eat their own hearts out, but in cases of ulcers this is exactly what they do with their stomachs. Such nourishment does not sustain for very long.

All life, plant and animal, depends on air and water. Animals depend on food from plants directly or from animals that in turn depend upon plants, but only rarely from animals that in turn depend on animals. In any case animals cannot do too much with the inorganic minerals and the immaterial light on which plants depend. Rooted in the soil and reaching toward the sun, plants render the inorganic organic and the immaterial material. What is life? Lots of light and dust.

One way to see the light is to eat it. "Fruit bears the closest relation to light," wrote Bronson Alcott, the transcendentalist friend of Thoreau. Dr. Bircher-Benner wrote that plants are biological accumulations of light and that nutritional energy is thus organized sunlight. His sanitarium just outside Zurich is quite near to Rudolf Steiner's Goetheanum near Basel. And Dr. Steiner wrote that the two products of animal digestion of plant foods are inner warmth and inner light. "Turn the spotlight inward," said Gandhi. People can be greedy over land or gluttonous over food growing on it, but there shall never be a shortage of light. "Light! More light!" were Goethe's last words from his death bed.

8. The Illogic of the Ecologic

The change which would be produced by simpler habits on political economy is sufficiently remarkable. The monopolizing eater of animal flesh would no longer destroy his constitution by devouring an acre at a meal, and many loaves of bread would cease to contribute to gout, madness, and apoplexy, in the shape of a pint of porter, or a dram of gin, when appeasing the long protracted famine of the hard-working peasant's hungry babies. The quantity of nutritious vegetable matter consumed in fattening the carcass of an ox would afford ten times the sustenance, undepraving indeed and incapable of generating disease if gathered immediately from the bosom of the earth.

PERCY SHELLEY
"A Vindication of Natural
Diet"

One way to make ends meet is to make meat end. Besides a cruelty, carnivorism is a superfluity. Like nicotine and alcohol, like caffeine and cholesterol, it is neither missed nor misused by those who never use it. The world economy would advance significantly if the growing seasons and growing pains devoted to the brewing of nutritionally-nil maté, coffee and tea; to the fermentation of subsequently ersatz barley, malt, and hops; to the burning of marijuana and tobacco; and to the sterilization of sugar and whitening of wheat, were all redirected to the cultivation of real food. In these terms flesh is only half real: a hectare of trees whose fruit is fed directly to people will fill far more hungry human mouths than a hectare of grass whose grain is fed to cattle whose flesh is fed to people. Since a moral issue hardly exists in picking tea leaves, harvesting hops, curing tobacco, or cutting cane, compared with slashing the throat of a lamb, the roots of vegetarianism reach deeper still, in fact all the way to the other side of the world. While Mary had a little lamb, and a little beef, and a little ham, another little girl in Africa, and a third young child in Asia, had next to nothing.

Chickens maintain a pecking order which they arrange and rearrange whenever fed. Sometimes they peck more than feed.

99

Humans also have a pecking order wherein the Western world feeds half on flesh while half the Eastern world half starves. The northern arctic supports almost total carnivores, while in the tropics flesh food is hardly known. But humans are ruled more by economy than geography. The wealthy in all societies eat more protein; the wealthy in wealthy societies eat more flesh. Today in continental China, high Party officials are nicknamed "Those who eat flesh."

Looking at the chickens, we see a small bird chased away from a crust of bread by a large bird. Then the large bird chases yet another away, and five more small chickens begin to peck at the unguarded bread. Enough is there for all seven; but no, the large one chases each away, one by one; by the time she is alone, the bread is gone. Wanting more than her share, she guards more but loses all. So shall it happen with humans. A world war might someday be fought over oil: not the kind poured into motors, but into mouths. Alternatives exist. For instance, Albert Schweitzer, in *The Ethics of Reverence for Life* tells the story of the crippled sparrow unable to compete with the flock for crumbs. So, the other sparrows, by mutual agreement, left those crumbs nearest it. Meanwhile Westerners continue to usurp their lion's share of the pork barrel.

Hortatory oratory against stomaching torture along with nurture is a dietary objection aimed at replacing animals and animal products with plants and plant products. Yet plants too are alive and feel pain, so if we are to avoid moral inconsistency we can aim at eating only products of plants, not plants themselves. Samuel Butler, in *Erewhon*, wrote a convincing chapter on vegetarianism, entitled "The Views of an Erewhonian Prophet Concerning the Rights of Animals," following it with a countering chapter concerning not carnivorism but the rights of vegetables.

> **It is not known whether the pain felt by ten trees equals that felt by one cow, or even whether any such pain can be measured.**

But . . . let us not give scientists any ideas for more research-and-destroy missions.

As a form of sustenance which does not grow from the ground but falls to the ground, fruit is possibly inadequate for many frozen in habits whose ice no thawing wind can crack, and it is certainly ill-advised for inhabitants of northerly cold climates. In the latter case, fruits in February are nearly as scarce in the market place as on a mountain peak. Only in the middle of Manhattan can melons from South America be bought in the middle of winter, and this does not take into account those who cannot afford the melons, or the fact that if melons were more important than money, neither is more important than health: we might be eating some of the best food in the world but would still be breathing some of the worst air.

Now those New Yorkers who worry about getting foods whole-sale as well as whole, might consider moving to Los Angeles; although its air is worse, at least its fruit is fresher and cheaper. This migration indeed appears to be the trend, though many decades will have to pass before New York becomes a city solely of carnivores. Likewise, an entire population's transition from carnivore to vegetarian would be just as gradual. Even if everyone renounced flesh overnight, initially the uneaten farm animals would continue eating plants, but eventually would disappear forever since no farmer will invest in a supply which has lost its demand. Once gone, their unborn offspring would burden no one, and proud farmers could no longer ask us to swallow their pride.

The ultimate knowledge of life is this: to desire nothing. Those who desire nothing out of life neither lust for life nor yearn for death; they arrive unconcerned, they depart uncaring. They try neither to forget nor to remember that out of which they appeared, they shall disappear. They confront the void but need never fill it with pretty trinkets and petty triumphs of everyday existence. Neither do they want their own life nor do they discard it, nor do they want or discard anyone else's. Many monks eat fish, but most eat no flesh. Carnivorism contrarily is the want of others' lives by those who want more than their own. From Sophocles to Heine, from Schopenhauer to Kierkegaard, from the Upanishads to Ecclesiastes and the Book of Job, the same thought has been repeated: sleep is good, death is better, never having been born is best.

But we must distinguish between dying and killing. No father claims the right to deliver his daughter to her tomb just because he had driven her from her mother's womb. The farmer who inseminates the cow cannot claim the right to incarcerate the calf. It is better that the cow and her calf never exist than that they endure the misery of the slaughterhouse. Life's quality must not be sacrificed to its quantity.

The fewer farm animals eaten by humans will mean the fewer plants eaten by farm animals; by killing fewer animals we therefore kill fewer, not more , plants. "The lips of the righteous feed many" (Proverbs 10:21). But, for several reasons, we must hesitate before emphatically advocating the ecological argument. First, if somehow the world were turned upside-down, if somehow north became south, right wrong, truth falsehood, good evil, and waste parsimony, if somehow outer economics were reversed, if somehow the vegetarian diet usurped more protein land than the carnivorous, inner ethics would still obligate us to eat like pigs rather than to eat pigs. Hence detailed discussion of this aspect of the subject is unwarranted, especially since the most popular paperback on vegetarianism in the 1970s, *Diet for a Small Planet*, elucidates this issue quite conclusively, indeed almost exclusively. A second objection to the ecological argument is that an entirely different conclusion can be drawn from its premises: not so much to omit flesh but to reorient the diet to depend primarily on yeast and algae as protein foods. Since the question here is of land, not life, the most worthy diet under these circumstances is one which requires no land. Yeast and algae are two such sources, easily grown yet hardly known.

Third, if the wasteful growing of condiment and crap crops were halted, carnivorism could continue for a century with the world economy unaltered. But no, ours is a society intent on shoving a cigarette in everyone's right hand and a drink in everyone's left, so that no one has a hand free with which to do anything either constructive or destructive, whichever seems more likely to be the case. Meanwhile, smoking a few leaves of a marijuana plant is still illegal in many places, while killing an animal is not.

The fourth objection is that the land-ration rationale is as blameworthy of the same selfishness as prohibiting human cruelty to animals only because it might foster human cruelty to humans. Some neighbors help extinguish fires only for fear they might spread to their own homes. If life is life, then equality must be established not just by elevating animals but by humbling humans. While we await the Copernicus to teach us that the earth does not revolve around ourselves, the ecological argument tries to convince us that animals are our enemies because they eat so much of our food. The tenuous tenet of *Diet for a Small Planet*—"lacto," "ovo," and "pisci" at that—is that for every human feeding off the fat of the lamb which in turn feeds off the food of the land, at least three vegetarians can feed directly off the food of the land. The planet might, indeed, support three times its present human carnivore population if it turned vegetarian, but someday when that population reached three times itself . . . then what? We can only conjecture what further adjustments will have to be made, for what is offered is only postponement, not atonement.

The fifth and final drawback sprouts from the fourth. Since a healthful vegetarian diet prolongs life, or at the least, postpones death, the many more people alive will also be living much longer. Less deaths to toll result in more mouths to feed, so that the entire argument is futile in not being fatal. Small potatoes for a small planet logically finds its fruition in Swift's "Modest Proposal," unless it restricts itself both morally and orally to a diet for a planet of the apes.

The five above answers to the ecological question are not above dispute, and unfortunately their relevant documentary evidence is meagre and vague. Nevertheless, the entire issue, despite all the scientific data on its side, can hardly be the most important reason for vegetarianism since it is essentially sociological, which is to say solely human oriented. Though hard to ignore, it is only an ornament added to the holiday tree and is hardly cause for celebration in itself. That tree's roots reach far deeper than the "six feet under" which society digs after most of our lifetimes, for that tree is the tree of life, the whole of life—and the whole of life includes death.

* * *

Our concerns are after all over matters of life *and* death. If we were to take the ecological position to its extreme, we would eat nothing so that others could eat something. Indeed, any argument for vegetarianism can be extended as well for starvation, but then so could any credentials for carnivorism be extended for cannibalism. Some who scoff at all our ideals sometimes point out that Hitler was at times a vegetarian; but at times so were this century's three great humanitarians: Gandhi, Schweitzer, and Einstein. Had Hitler not been even a sporadic vegetarian, perhaps concentration camp ovens would have produced not just soap, but soup. Where people are treated like animals, they can very easily be eaten like animals. Fortunately, Hitler did not often eat animals.

We kill to live, but the less we kill the more we live. Green plants, blessed, are free of all ill karma, but green is seen in animals only in the eyes. Deprived of chlorophyll, we choose between either killing ourselves that others might live or killing others that we might live, and then in degree for whatever choice. Or we can completely wash our hands of the matter and a million microbes known only to God are mercilessly dumped down the drain like so many Satans hurled from heaven.

While washing their hands in preparation for vivisection, few scientists lament their million human guinea pigs and none their million million guinea pig guinea pigs. We kiss guinea pigs and gerbils as pets, but kill mice and rats as pests. We consider squirrels friendly and cuddly, but rats filthy and ugly. Is the difference in the texture of their tails or in the teller of their tales? Unable to protect wild animals from shotguns and traps, instead we protect ourselves with blindfolds and earplugs. The vegetable man shouts the price of corn but never whispers stories of the raccoon hunt the month before: in one night by a full moon three hunters and their twenty-four dogs stalked forty raccoons up six trees, and within a month all the raccoons were hats and coats . . . all because raccoons eat corn too.

Though no referendum was held at the polls nor contribution ever sought at the streetcorner, everyone participates in the hunt merely by living in a society which has not yet outworn its hunting skins. The predatory nature of primitive humans cannot be denied; even modern humans, calling themselves sportsmen and hunters, persist as predators. Their anachronistic actions turn an otherwise deadly serious affair into a game, for many do not eat what they kill. Thus some hunters might be vegetarians, though only hypothetically: vegetarianism is concerned not merely with eating and not eating, but with killing and not killing.

Many athletes are vegetarians, and the best athletes often are; sportsmen, the more violent athletes, only occasionally are; but the best boxers and football players, the most violent never are. Hence, the unique meat punching bag in the film "Rocky." Muhammad Ali confided to Dick Gregory the wish to become a vegetarian someday, believing it impossible to do while still a boxer. Team sports are essentially surrogate hunts involving two tribes in competition for the "game." Hence the "pigskin" in football. Meanwhile, the less active male majority, still predatorily inclined, recline on Sunday sofas, lackadaisical as lions after a kill, belching beer and gobbling hero sandwiches, and watch others' games distantly through twentieth-century television sets. Thus the hunt persists.

Raccoons could be poisoned or trapped, but are as often hunted. Perhaps, besides mice, they are the chief competitors among mammals in the field for our crops. This makes them the most like ourselves, so we shoot them with what we most kill ourselves. When we aim to kill large numbers of people we do so with large guns: cannons and mortars, pom-poms and missiles. We have certainly evolved as drastically in warfare as in dinnerware: the same technology which produced the atomic bomb has brought us the microwave oven.

Our military armaments in many ways reflect our dietary developments. Mammals in general began first as insect eaters like their reptilian forebears; a rare few have survived as insectivores, while the others became herbivores, nearly complete carnivores or omnivores; a rarer few were then transformed a second time, for instance, humans from herbivores to carnivores. Only humans among all other species of mammals changed yet again, beginning as reptilian insectivores, progressing to simian herbivores, evolving to primatial carnivores, and so far concluding as omnivores, which dubiously if not deviously, but anyhow bluntly, have here been spoken of as carnivores. Anthropologists view this third step from carnivore to omnivore as one of the great changes which make us distinctly *human*. Either this change is not great enough, or, if it is great, we are preparing for a greater fourth change to make us *humane:* omnivore back to herbivore.

The whole of our history as nearly complete carnivores is short, and as omnivores shorter still, compared to other developments of ourselves and of other animals. Whereas other animals would have waited to acquire fangs and claws to become carnivores, humans simply devised clubs and spears. As humans we have some independence from the body; for gathering food, we rely not on a surprise attack but on a charge card. Like buyers on credit who have few problems returning merchandise since they have not yet paid for it, our hasty evolution actually makes for an easier return to complete herbivorism since our bodies are still made for it. Yet, some will always find ways of making purchases, whether they need anything or not, so the best thing for them may just be to have no money in their pockets. Likewise with carnivores: the best thing for them may just be to have no flesh in their markets. If people ate raccoon flesh, the killing and the eating would not be the issue here; rather, the consideration would be the three hunters and their twenty-four dogs killing the raccoons for them.

Raccoon hunts or no, our vegetables and fruits are chemically sprayed, so everyone kills insects. No one can wash leaves clean of all their aphids or pick grains clear of all their larvae; thus those who eat organically and so do not eat insecticides, instead eat insects. Whether we kill the insects and eat the plants, or kill insects and eat insects, the road of return from omnivore to herbivore leads to yet another return: herbivòre back to insectivore. Or we might even attempt to live on the organic material in mud, as does the earthworm.

Beyond vegetarianism, beyond veganism, beyond fruitarianism, beyond insectivorism, beyond even limivorism, we can try to live on sunshine, air, and water. Try as we might to settle at eating only fruits and killing no plants, we will still kill insects. It should be emphasized that establishing our dietary history presents many knotty problems, and not all students of this study have arrived at the same conclusions. This admittedly recondite reasoning for insectivorism is perhaps as sterile as fruit from the fumatory; if so, we can ponder only so far until answers fall past our comprehension. Can vegetarianism be considered truly a step beyond? Beyond what? And how can it be proved so? It is not just at the dinner table that vegetarians set themselves apart from carnivores. Vegetarians who have returned to carnivorism have admitted to feeling a part of the rest of humanity again. But the point is precisely not to feel unity with only humanity, but with the whole of nature.

Natural food stores are often named "The Good Earth," "Down to Earth," and "Back to Nature," or combinations thereof. Getting back to nature corresponds more with cutting out flesh than cutting into it because, though some flesh is prepared without nitrites and some animals are raised without stilbestrol, few animals are fed completely organically. As with the natural food diet, the raw food regimen is also generally vegetarian since few Westerners devour raw flesh. At first all our foods, ranging from fruits and nuts to grubs and worms, were eaten raw. Humans probably first cooked only as carnivores. Since cooking vegetables is a practice probably borrowed from cooking flesh, once we have ceased eating flesh, we should stop cooking altogether. Nevertheless, certain cooking systems do seem to benefit their adherents, so we must appraoch the raw facts with a grain of kelp.

The ecological responsibility claimed for eating plants rather than animals must also be asserted for eating the same plants raw rather than cooked. We need and therefore eat far less of a vegetable raw than cooked because, when eaten raw, we get more. Flesh roasted over grills half feeds the flames, just as vegetables boiled in water half nourish the drains. But a sun-ripened fruit which never is tested by trials of fire and water voluntarily confesses all, so long as we approach it with the tooth, and nothing but the tooth. Some primitive tribes represented God by the sun and the Devil by fire. Contemporaneously we represent rationality by radiancy.

Prometheus, who gave humans fire, must also have taught what to do with it, for instance, how to use it to render flesh more pleasing to the taste. He was punished for this by having his vitals eternally devoured by vultures. Shelley tells us these vultures are metaphors for disease. This explains then the enervation of generations of our ancestors who, chained to the rock of salt, have been frying and boiling and baking and broiling, and have had problems equally with their livers as with their lives. It amounts to this: cooked cabbage may or may not be more nourishing than its accompanying corn beef, but raw cabbage is certainly more so than either the cooked cabbage or the cooked beef.

Two marks of our human evolution were made when we cooked flesh and planted seeds. We might evolve higher by not cooking flesh and again planting our own seeds, and higher still by not eating flesh and not cooking seeds. Most of us are urbanites, so growing our own food is nearly as impossible as living our own lives. Urbanite or not, anyone can sprout seeds, grains, beans, and even nuts, and eat the sprouts raw. Just as more food is gotten from grain fed directly to humans than from the same grain fed to cattle which are fed to humans, and just as more nutrition is gotten from vegetables served raw than cooked, far more food and nutrition are gotten from sprouted seeds, grains, and beans than unsprouted. We might not necessarily grow the original seeds, but neither do the apple farmers whose trees were begun by Grandpa Johnny.

Lao-tse said unawareness of the feet is the sign of a pair of shoes that fits, and of the waist of a belt that fits; so should we say unawareness of the body is the criterion of a diet that fits. The giant redwoods live for hundreds of years, and if they have any one purpose it is photosynthesis. The human body is a temple whose walls must be buttressed as strong as the mighty redwood. Thus its single congregant might find long refuge for the years necessary to fulfill its real single purpose—understanding. Perhaps, for some, vegetables are not as palatable raw as cooked; but to whom is the body as pleasurable diseased as healthy?

Growing our own food teaches patience and gratitude—hence humility—and assures freshness and wholesomeness—hence health. When a raja who had ruled thousands of Indians aspired to rule solely himself, he retired to a small plot of his former estate and ate only those foods grown with his own hands. Not all of us own land for gardens, but most have window sills and cupboards where we can grow our own sprouts. "He who cultivates barley," sings the Zoroastrian hymn, "cultivates righteousness." Thomas Jefferson understood this in intending to frame his nation's future around the farmer. Monks will often spend as much time tending their gardens as their souls, and shamans in some societies do nothing but pray for rain.

Concern to eat nutritious food should be as great as an intention to live a healthy life, but neither of these is as important as the quest for knowledge and wisdom. If, as the elderly so often instruct the young, wisdom comes with age, then the longer we live the wiser we should become. "Does not the ear try words as the palate tastes food? Wisdom is with the aged, and understanding in length of days" (Job 12:11–12). Though food makes no one wise, food makes us live, and life makes us wise.

Perhaps only the squirrel who first ate acorns is wise enough to answer whether the acorn or the oak grew first. Or perhaps only the human who first ate squirrels is wise enough. The Edenic tree of knowledge either coincidentally bore apples, or the apple tree accidentally bore knowledge. Either way, the more direct way of getting at the root of knowledge is to eat apples, not animals that eat apples. "'Tis well said," concludes Voltaire's *Candide*. "But we must cultivate our gardens."

9. The Problem of Being a Flesh Eater (with No Idea of the Problem)

You ask me why Pythagoras abstained from eating meat. For my part I wonder what was the disposition, idea, or motive of the first man who put to his mouth a thing slaughtered and touched with his lips the flesh of a dead animal . . . Actually, the reasons why those primitive people first started the eating of flesh was probably their utter poverty.

PLUTARCH
"The Eating of Meat"

Asked why he did not eat meat, George Bernard Shaw answered that that is putting the cart before the horse and in turn asked: "Why *do* you eat meat?" But the one with whom he spoke remained silent. What carnivore can list as many reasons for the necessity of flesh eating as we have done for its superfluity? What philosopher has written a convincing tract for the cause of carnivorism? What poet has lamented the misunderstood lives of the butcher and the executioner? What prophet has bewailed his people's worship of the golden carrot? So, how does it come to pass that carnivorism is such an omnipresent part of the Western and, particularly, the American diet? We, with Plutarch, must ask, "Just why do people eat meat?"

The three mainsprings that have perpetuated carnivorism are tradition, imitation, and sensation. Concerning the third, what tastes good to one person cannot be disputed by another. One person's meat is another's vegetarianism. If flesh tastes good, then what is valid for the carnivore is simply vapid for the vegetarian. Not much more can be said about sensation, so to tradition and imitation we shall devote the balance of this discussion. Tradition: one's parents ate it, so one eats it, and one's children eat it. Imitation: everyone else eats it, so one wants to be the same as everyone else; everyone tells one to eat it, so one does as one is told.

Of all members of the animal kingdom, humanity is the least ruled by instinct: hence it's ruling the animal kingdom. Freedom from instinct is at times an advantage and at other times a hindrance. Synonymous with potential for change, this freedom makes precarious the wisdom ancestors learned through trial and error, through take and mistake. Thus humans first ate flesh even though they did not have the guts to do it nor even the intestines. If just one generation fails in preserving the proper tradition but instead introduces a detrimental one, the whole of humanity can suffer for thousands of years.

The hand which winds the mainsprings of tradition and imitation is indoctrination. An illiterate, primitive culture communicates orally, while a literate, technological one does so through media. The long-literate West abounds with its media machinery, so to trace the cause of its heavy carnivorism we need not excavate any archaeological site, but need only read its newspapers, listen to its radios, watch its televisions, and glance at its billboards. Either we, like everyone else, will become indoctrinated into carnivorism, or we, more like ourselves, will become wary of it and might thereby expose it. This is not to say that carnivorism was introduced by the television; however, no Western culture makes either so large a part of its meals. Both are made possible by affluence, which in turn is responsible for advertisements, which in turn see to it that our affluence is quickly expended. As yet no such thing exists as the vegetarian TV dinner.

The prophet Daniel resolved not to defile himself with the king's rich food and wine, and wished instead to be given vegetables and water. That he proved himself healthier for it is not the point; where we must take his example is his willingness to defy the king. Many are easily affected by the whims of an influential few, while many simply follow where custom directs, horses at the end of a tether hardly inquiring after effects, hardly caring about causes.

Those who follow only the well-trodden path, who never think of the means toward their unconcerned end, who neither act out their thoughts nor think out their actions, can nevertheless be good and kind. Maybe as many as half of all the Mr. Chuck Steaks and Ms. Virginia Hams in this world would refrain from eating flesh if they had to kill the cows and pigs themselves. Asceticism is not the issue here: it is not wrong that something tastes good, or that eating gives pleasure. But it is wrong when one's pleasure must depend on another's pain.

Several years ago a drunken party of Brazilian hunters ventured into the Amazon jungle and slaughtered a small tribe of Indians. This was no new event, but for some unknown reason this particular case was brought to court and to world view. The drunkards were tried for murder but acquitted since the judge held them irresponsible: the party did not consider the Indians to be humans but animals. Therefore he deemed they be tried for killing animals . . . which was no crime according to the law. They were therefore reprimanded, instructed that Indians *are* humans, and dismissed. If Brazilian justice had been followed, all those on trial at Nuremburg would have been exonerated.

Had they first stumbled on a flock of geese or a family of monkeys, the hunters might never have killed the Indians. Hemingway said he killed animals instead of killing himself. (But he still, finally, killed himself.) The confusion of treating humans as animals merely affirms the humanity of animals and the bestiality of humans. During that terrible European era of Nazism, Jews and Poles were often transported to concentration camps in cattle cars. Yet, to this day, cattle are still transported to slaughterhouses in cattle cars. Though it is deplorable that humans were treated as animals, it is also terrible that animals are still treated "as animals." Jewish survivors of the death camps predominantly became vegetarians—because they knew what it was to be treated as animals.

Nine million people were exterminated in concentration camps throughout Europe in one decade; presently, nine million animals are daily executed in American slaughterhouses. Germans in communities near the camps contended they had no idea what went on inside, or at least they had no proof of it. Similarly, most Americans have no idea of what goes on in slaughterhouses, since their only proof is well-hidden in their milk puddings and their mince pies. Those with some idea of what might be seen nevertheless have never seen it. People cannot be expected to go out of their way to seek something, especially when every device to keep them unaware is employed by those who stand to profit from collective ignorance. How does this occur? A crowded city street is being prepared for widening, and everyone responsible for the road's congestion thinks it a great shame to see that the row of trees along the road is being marked for destruction. Some circulate petitions, or send outraged letters to editors, or march with protest signs: the petitions are written on paper, the letters printed on newspaper, the signs painted on cardboard—all from trees. But few feel sorrow for these trees; these trees grew in forests far away from city sight. Few comprehend the connection between a seedling crushed under heel and a scrap of paper tossed into the gutter, between towering pines and the Sunday New York *Times*.

Likewise with flesh and the animal from which it is severed. People say they love animals, but the animals they love are only dogs and cats, not calves and lambs. Perhaps the dichotomy is due simply to duplicity, but people relegate farm animals into a different class from family pets. This distinction rests neither upon human intelligence, nor upon human contention of the animals' supposed lack of it. Inconsistency carried to the extreme of incoherency is the only excuse for being disgusted by the eating of horse flesh but not by the eating of cow flesh. Do caretakers who feed their pets pork know that the hog is more intelligent than any cat or dog?

Suppose we return a few years later to that widening road, now a superhighway. Every morning heaps of smashed bodies on its pavement act as immobile answers to the eternal question "Why did the chicken cross the road?" Having not gotten to the other side of the road, but rather the other side of life, they are removed by highway maintenance crews well before morning rush hour traffic. But animals will throughout the day make the road their dead end. Passing motorists confronted with the carnage sincerely feel pity, even at 100 km/h, as they return home to consume carcasses killed by no accident. Where is the logic, and where the justice?

People hardly ponder over pigs when they eat a pork chop, or over cows when they eat a hamburger, or upon the slaughterhouse when they eat a porterhouse. Maintaining this coverture are the many crews employed by the flesh industries which tidy up every roadway between the slaughterhouse and the market place. These roads are everywhere; we all live on one. We could view this ignorance as irremissible, and take it upon ourselves to expose the otherwise obscured atrocities. Unable to bring an audience to the abattoir, we might bring an abattoir to the audience: the most widely distributed film on the subject is "The Blood of the Beasts," a short documentary of a Paris slaughterhouse, by Georges Franju. Often shown in college film programs, its intelligent, sensitive audiences are of course horrified. Yet few see the connection between what they view and what they chew: after the film the same students sleepwalk to the same snackbars to swallow the same hamburgers, seasoned with much catsup but no compunction.

In the case of human abuse of animals, when the facts are pre-

sented, people react with disbelief, disaffection . . . or vegetarianism. The facts have been disclosed in various vegetarian
and humanitarian polemics, but carnivorism somehow persists.
Galileo's contemporaries hesitated to peer through his telescope
not because they feared seeing Jupiter's moons, but because the
sight would have shaken their illusion of geocentricity. More
is at stake than the carnivores' comfort should they visit a
slaughterhouse; their whole diet might subsequently change, and
that is a larger part of daily habit than most are willing to
modify. Few eaters of flesh want to know that animals die painfully, or that they die at all; in fact few seem to know animals
even live. Knowing everything about braising beef, few know
anything about raising cattle.

Patron ignorance is further enforced by the location of slaughterhouses in isolated rural areas. The major exception is Chicago,
once the "hog butcher of the world," now mostly for Illinois.
Flesh merchants can ship live cows across state lines unharassed,
but dead ones must pass federal inspection. Thus Armour has
redistributed its forces to dozens of smaller armories across the
country so that it must meet only the less stringent state laws.
Pigeons, blessed with wings that they could escape the butcher
knife, now occupy the old Chicago slaughterhouses. Wheat,
spilled from the feed cars, now grows along the railroad tracks.
The bone yard has been bulldozed over. And one by one, the
buildings, where so many millions of animals fell victims to
slaughter crews, are now falling victims to wrecking crews. At
least a dozen large flesh refinery factories still operate in the area,
but otherwise the notorious Union Stockyard is now an "in-
dustrial park." By 1984, the only reminder of the jungle will be
the entrance gate, designated an historic landmark—by Mayor
Daley.

The gate very closely resembles that of another historic site:
Dachau, now a mausoleum museum. The buildings, the barbed
wire, the ovens where hundreds of Hansels were burned, the
showers where thousands of Gretels were gassed, all are recon-
structions. In a yard where people were shot in target practice,
flowers now flourish: as any modern farmer knows, blood is an
excellent fertilizer. Just as flesh for city markets comes mostly
from slaughterhouses in rural areas, though its inmates worked
in many factories of nearby Munich the concentration camp was
located near only the small community of Dachau. Dead bodies
are best buried in basements, where few go and where the light is
dim.

Visitors need not be Jewish to sense the doom lingering in the

Dachau air even to this day. But why is it only some people sense that same doom today at the Union Stockyards? Easterners would attribute this to blocked chakras, Westerners to blocked nasal passages. Yet no matter from what direction we look, the greatest block is in our field of vision. What the merchants of venison conceal through obfuscation is one thing; what they choose to reveal through advertisement is quite another. Consumers still believe animals are raised in arboreal dells of bucolic tranquility, where the sheep are herded by Timmy and Lassie, where the chickens scamper playfully outside the front porch and peck at Gramps' feet as he tosses them their feed, and where the cows are tenderly milked by Mom.

Mass media and the advertising enterprises to which they owe their existences reinforce the erroneous education of the orectic consumer. Scholars, students, poets, and philosophers have long known that vegetarianism is humanity's natural way of life, but the omniscient influence of cattle barons and worshippers of gold and calves has obscured the carnage of carnivorism. Wealth has won over health. Every time a piece of flesh is paid for, another penny is added to the industry's coffers to propagandize its cause. But whenever a bunch of carrots or kilogram of soybeans is bought, every penny saved is merely withheld: though not thrown into hell, neither does it ascend into heaven.

The West has become a herd of sheep led by blind and blinding shepherds, a race of people hardly different from what they eat. Old shepherds led by staff and dog, new ones by advertising and indoctrination. "Woe to the shepherds who destroy and scatter the sheep of my pasture, says the Lord," (Jeremiah 23:1). At Dachau—and for all that is known, still at Karaganda—civilized people were held captive by barbarians bred by a society whose weapons of incarceration were barbed wire and machine guns; now the weapons are radio and television, and humans are exploited economically by those who have gained experience abusing animals bodily.

Perhaps the chemical hormones injected into the flesh of exploited animals in turn affect the humans eating it, for instance to become exploitable so that they will believe they must indeed eat and therefore exploit animals. Yet, this is where humans differ from animals: the great mystery of the will to live is animals' allowing themselves to be so exploited and yet persisting in living; whereas humans often resort to suicide or willed starvation, given the same circumstances. In a line of Jews to be shot was a young mother, one child in her arms and another in her womb.

The Nazi soldier in the firing squad opposite where she stood whispered to her that when the shooting began he would not fire upon her, and that she should fall down and feign death. "Shoot me!" she begged.

The difference between humans and animals is most marked in our unique ability to despise ourselves. If one must first love oneself to love others, then also one must first despise oneself to despise others. No wonder the American government, through the gauntleted hand of the USDA, encourages carnivorism. Nebraska Senator Carl Curtis in 1975 criticized vegetarianism during a Senate debate concerning cattle-feed additives, saying: "In the whole history of the world, whenever a meat-eating race has gone to war against a non-meat-eating race, the meat-eating race has won." If true, what was intended as censure when spoken to his peers actually amounts to praise when heard by our ears. No government wants gentle armies; anyone who allows even unwilling servitude in the armed forces is no less exploited than a horse or a hog or a cow; the difference is that the beef cow is slaughtered after two years, whereas the drafted soldier, if he survives combat, will be set free.

We have already seen in Chapter 6 how flesh eaters assimilate the traits either of other fierce flesh-eating animals or of the docile farm animals whose flesh they eat. Tartars, famous for ferocity and for feeding on excessive amounts of flesh, illustrate the first case. Yet those who desire to be as fierce as Tartars, who wish to be conquerors rather than conquered, merely reflect exploitation by the State, and illustrate the second case. Although Tartars charging on the backs of horses would easily overpower Buddhists meditating beneath bodhi trees, to whom would we attribute the greater wisdom? To the Tartar, as stupid as his horse? Or to the Buddha, as solemn as his tree? When not depicted meditating, the Buddha is shown laughing. The meek shall inherit the mirth.

The harbinger humans who first killed each other with clubs learned the trick and perfected the technique from killing quarry. The first few minutes of the film "2001" illustrate this precisely. Not only did humanity become warriors after becoming carnivores, but world peace shall remain unattainable until we all again become vegetarians. Now, announcing that flesh eating induces aggressiveness is not the point here, nor should it be anywhere: quite the contrary, it is best kept quiet, for some people are of such inferior character that they would devour flesh for that very purpose. In the late 1800s, an evangelist roamed frontier America preaching against the evils of flesh, attributing its use to stirring up the passions. Everywhere he rode, its eating increased.

The majority of humanity quietly and unobtrusively tends to its personal affairs, unmoved either by pleas for benevolence or by demands for violence. Provoked, however, it will be stirred. The whale and leopard boycotts of the 1970s attest to this. If the plight of a nearly extinct species arouses public sentiment, then the next small step is recognition that each individual animal of any species represents an entity as distinct and irreplaceable as the species itself. The blood-and-thunder coverage of and commotion over the seal slaughters in Norway and Canada demonstrated such concern for individuals whose species was not so near extinction. Tuna fishers follow dolphins to find schools of tuna and, for several years until newer nets were developed, they captured and killed both, but canned only the tuna. (Who knows? Maybe they canned both.) On these terms, many people, outraged about killing dolphins, refused to eat tuna; the next step is to nurture outrage about killing tuna; and, on these terms, the step after that is to refuse to eat tuna. In 1976, a controversy arose between England and Iceland concerning fishing rights. Let us forget about such rights of England, and such rights of Iceland; let us consider the rights of fish.

Still, Englishmen and Icelanders, fishermen and canners, eaters of dolphins and of tunas, have rights. No hate should be felt for carnivorous humans any more than against carnivorous animals. We should not compel a human not to kill an animal. We cannot prohibit murder of animals nor, were there such laws, could we form a gendarmerie to enforce them. Yet the cry against the false bliss of ignorance and the death kiss of insouciance should never cease. To this purpose the individual must be the watchdog, but need never bite; loud barks usually suffice to destroy institutionalized ignorance, which quickly flees our flashlights like a black cat in the night.

Our fight is as much for information as against misinformation. For instance, the misconception of the life of the calf. If only some people knew that veal is white not because the calf is milk-fed, as is popularly believed, but because it has been bred anemic, immobile, and in the dark! Since half of all calves are males who cannot gain admittance into the land of milk and money, without a veal industry the milk industry could be only half as large, and milk would be twice the price. Farm families who make their living from the daily milk made by their dairy cows, know the true price which must be paid; thus many do not eat veal, abstaining from what they know, but embracing what they do not know . . . since they do eat other sorts of flesh. In these matters the typical carnivore generally knows nothing . . . and eats everything.

Ignorance is due more to the institutions for which humans are responsible than to the humans themselves. Perpetuation of the ignorance is one of the major functions of these institutions, once they become established. Through the media, the flesh industries have encouraged narcose sensibilities in audiences by humanizing the consumed so as not to dehumanize the consumers. Hence, Charlie the Tuna tries his hardest to get canned and, just the opposite, little children sing of wishing they were wieners "because then everyone would love me." But one child in the crowd is too clever and sings he is glad he is not a wiener "or there would be nothing left of me."

Making eaten animals into people, and making people wish they were eaten animals, merely signifies an underlying condition for carnivorism: its substitute for cannibalism. A brand name for a Virginia Ham is "Hansel and Gretel"; it is well known what the witch wished to do with them. But not so well known is the real reason they were lost in the forest. For this we must consult the Grimm's fairy tale, not the Humperdinck opera. It occurs that their cruel mother had not enough to feed her whole family, and so sent them away into the woods to starve to death so she and her husband would have enough to eat for themselves. Obviously, the witch suffered from the same famine and solved her problem in her own solitary fashion. This tale parallels the way dairy farmers deal with veal.

Our human story might very well reach its end in an oven such as the one intended for Hansel but which instead swallowed up the witch. Quite distinct from the oven is the garden, and that is where our story began with Adam and Eve, not with their creation, but with their transgression. The links between Adam and Eve, and Hansel and Gretel, are Cain and Abel. When Cain (a tiller of the ground) saw Abel (a keeper of sheep) sacrifice an animal, he assumed killing was good; it is well known what Cain did to Abel—but it was Abel, not Cain, who was the first killer. Hence the first killer human became the first human killed.

* * *

Whether humans will ever cease killing other humans depends on whether humans will ever cease killing animals, and that depends on whether humans will ever cease eating animals.

Given a year, few new vegetarians again desire flesh; such a desire is an impure thought brought forth by impure food, in this case the flesh itself. As long as it is constantly fed, an unhealthy appetite is hardly ever satiated. Upon waking in the morning after a late night steak dinner, one develops the hunger for a breakfast of bacon and eggs. Desires, especially those against which no effort is exerted, easily become vices. Oscar Wilde advised that the best way to overcome a vice is to succumb to it; perhaps this proves effective for some, but too many squander their entire lives succumbing.

For many, flesh eating is a pleasure. But it is the pleasure of Dionysius whose swords of Damocles hang over dining room chairs by the hairs of the very animals whose flesh is eaten. Are there not greater pleasures at less risk? If truly carnivorous, humans would delight more in raw flesh than ripe fruit, and would feel more at peace in an abattoir than in an orchard. Quite the contrary, only disguise and disinfectant make flesh palatable. It is dressed in nearly everything except clothing, and is pickled and peppered, spiced and salted, roasted and fried, pattied and pied, foiled and broiled, simmered and stewed, in short eaten every way but whole and raw, and doctored so those who devour it might be called "civilized." Even when raw, flesh is disguised with sodium nitrates and nitrites, which conceal the gangrenous sight and stench of putrefaction.

Since carnivores neither see nor go near a slaughterhouse, nor wish to, what do they see? Only the supermarket facade of glareless glass and stainless steel. Customers who request observation of the cutting room are refused; managers excuse themselves saying insurance does not cover visitors, or company policy prohibits entry. "It is for your own protection," one manager replied. He seemed to mean sanitation, but also implied innocence and ignorance.

The greatest masquerade of all lurks within the lexicon: the disingenuous designation of *flesh* as *meat* is but the beginning of society's other self-aggrandizing fictions. According to what cryptogram does "flesh" become "meat?" Imagine a hamburger: in that is nothing offensive to the average carnivore. Imagine just the flesh without a bun: in that is nothing offensive. Imagine the chopped flesh still raw and not yet shaped into a patty: in that is nothing offensive. Imagine the chopped flesh still sitting in cellophane on the supermarket shelf: in that is nothing offensive. Imagine the flesh still a chunk: in that is nothing offensive. Imagine the chunk uncarved from the carcass: well, here might be something offensive; here some feel squeamish looking at the split and stripped body of something half recognizable as an animal, or recognizable as half an animal. Imagine the whole dead body, uneviscerated and unskinned: here indeed is much to lose repose over; few really wish to see large dead animals; small fish and chickens are enough. Imagine the steer at the eternal moment of death, throat cut by a cutthroat, leg broken by a shackle, and hoisted upside down: this few wish to see. Imagine the animal alive meandering around its crowded pen: suddenly all is past the point of insult or injury; once again here is nothing offensive.

The flesh industry is all too aware of what its consumers want to eat and want not to see of what they eat.

What consumers want not to see, the industry will be the last to show them. Most people think of only the first stage when they imagine a hamburger, and of only the last stage if they wonder from where it comes: somehow everything unseemly between is forgotten and unseen. The packers are not to be blamed for not showing the process by which they render their product, for none are proud of it; but besides hiding behind facades, they fabricate falsehoods. Advertisements entice us to smoke this brand of cigarette, or to drink that brand of alcohol, or this coffee or that tea. The more organized organ grinders, however, advertise simply to eat flesh. Occasionally we see Cancer Society and Alcoholic Anonymous admonitions; only recently have vegetarian activist campaigns begun to inform the unknowing of the pernicious properties of flesh. We have far to advance, considering that as recently as the turn of the century, tobacco was heralded as healthful.

Our materialistic civilization consists of but two classes of citizens: not aristocracy and peasants, not masters and slaves, not military and civilians, not even politicians and populace, and certainly not scholars and students, but rather producers and consumers. While producers are also consumers, all the other consumers are not producers. In order to proceed with business in the flesh market without hindrance from their own consciences or from others' criticisms, the two form a silent partnership. Consumers do not wish to be reminded of the lives of the animals whose flesh they eat; producers do not wish to remind them. And while packaging shapes the product to suit consumer desires, advertising shapes consumer desires to fit the product.

City people remain almost totally ignorant of the methods undertaken by animal undertakers to place flesh in the picnic casket. The little they suspect, they conveniently forget. Modern farms are factories whose production lines assemble animal bodies to be disassembled in the slaughterhouse. Depictions of de-beaked broiler hens imprisoned in moribund darkness would hardly sell the products of Colonel Sanders and Frank Perdue. Factory farmers and flesh packers never acknowledge cruelty: obviously those who keep their stock in bonds are more interested in Wall Street's stocks and bonds. In this particular industry, evil is the root of all money.

So long as they fatten, this is pointed to as proof that the animals are content with their lot. Who can be trusted to maintain at least humane conditions where there should be nothing to maintain at all? What government can be respected whose existent animal welfare laws exclude livestock and whose few laws concerning them are out-of-date? Assurances that the well fed is the well bred are heard from officials on only one side of the fence, the side whose dollars are greener. To them, vegetarians are faddists, cultists, or just plain nuts, while humanitarians towards animals are anarchists or extreme misanthropes. As it is, the only regular and widespread access to information we have is the industry's own propaganda, and these views begin at the mendacious and end at the ridiculous.

Much free information is available from the USDA directly, or indirectly from dozens of flesh industry associations that stock its publications. This simple fact in itself warrants no accusations, for as much is done for soybeans and radishes; however, the nature and magnitude of the materials are astonishing. For instance, the Yearbook of Agriculture, *That We May Eat*, comes compliments of one's congressperson. The language of the 1975 edition reveals the official USDA attitude that animals are servitors of the human race, machines whose function is to convert plant food to flesh food. Page 123 states: ''They [cattle] will convert crop residues . . . into beef and milk for human consumption.'' Page 125 continues: ''Only three decades ago Americans depended on countless backyard flocks to provide them with chicken for the table. Today, however, broiler production is industrialized in much the same way as the production of cars, shoes, or TV sets.'' Page 133 tells us: ''The hog is a rapid, prolific, and relatively efficient meat-making machine." And then we are fed outright lies on page 126: "Today's broiler . . . is fed better, housed and cared for better, and pampered in many ways." Incarceration and overcrowding of chickens is described on page 132 as " . . . intimate contact with his peers."

The largest and most influential of all organ organizations is the American Meat Institute. In *All About the AMI*, on page 13, the author sets forth its function as " . . . supplying pertinent material . . . to schools, libraries, home economists, rural and urban organizations, and thought leaders throughout the nation." To this purpose an inquirer will be given many free booklets and papers. One such request was answered by a financial report throughout which animals are described as "raw materials."

The power of the word extends far and wide, molding thought, holding imagination, and commanding action. The English language has loaded its crafts of communication with many disguises. What is called "fleisch" for both animals and humans in German, is called "meat" and "flesh" in English. Animals have "hides," but people possess "skin." Such separation must occur before blood can flow. More extreme is war, where the human enemy must be reduced lower than animals to the level of inanimate objects. For example, a general discussing nuclear strike capabilities never once implied killing and slaughter but instead spoke of "overpressures," "blast parameters," "temperature threshholds," and "fallout interfaces."

Society's most strictly tabooed subjects are those that reveal the negative side of life, and for the West the most odious aspect of life is death. It is hidden not just under two meters of fertile earth, but often inside two pages of fine print. Thus, what flesh advertisements consciously seem to mean camouflages what they subconsciously mean to mean. Our idealized views of ourselves are reflected through the media mirror; those mirrors which show sights we do not wish to see, we simply cover.

The AMI is the first to uphold the death taboo, as we see easily in their advertisements. One series of these, old but classic, was run in monthly installments between 1950 and 1954 in two leading popular intellectual periodicals, "Harper's" and "Atlantic." The series presents a facetious facade of smiling animals, even when on their way to market. Paradoxically, animals are also portrayed as a sort of enemy that requires "costly feeds." Animals are not even acknowledged as raised; rather, "meat is grown." "Raw materials are converted by livestock into America's favorite protein food." Meat packers thus deal "in buying livestock and selling it as meat," while animals are no more than a "storehouse of meat, on the hoof." But the consumer "doesn't want a whole critter on the hoof;" rather, he wants "to convert him into steaks and roasts for his home freezer." So, "next time you eye a meat animal, look at the eatin' parts." "Millions of youngsters and millions of oldsters, once excluded from the market for meat by fallacious dietary theories, are now in there pitching with their table tools." The AMI rejoices, since "while just about everybody likes the idea of meat on the table, most folks also like the idea of turning the processing and curing chore over to the nation's meat packers." After all, "you want just ham—not a whole hog." According to the AMI, not only do we need meat, but we need leather. "So it's a good thing for all of us that ours is a country of meat eaters." To better supply these needs for both leather and meat, the cattleman takes the cattle from grazing and imprisons them in lots where they are grain-fed: "He takes them to his beef factory and feeds them—fills out their frames," giving them "the kind of living that his boarders enjoy." But until what point? Well, the destiny of pigs is more descriptive: "They spend the summer and early fall growing to pork-chop size." "Summertime is always the time when a new meat crop is growing up." And then in the fall, "Pigs come into a packing plant in one piece; they leave in as many as eighty different pork products."

These advertisements are old and were found by deliberate research. More recently and randomly are found those broadcast on radio and television or printed in newspapers. Rather than enumerating the many—for such a task would be even more boring to read than to write—two people spent a day watching two different television channels, listening to two different radio stations, and thumbing through two different newspapers, in order to sample the few. The day chosen was April 11, the anniversary of the liberation of Buchenwald.

Although many fleshy dog and cat food commercials appeared, the two televisions yielded no fleshy human food messages that day. The radios each offered one, both from Perdue chickens and narrated by its preacher president, Frank Perdue. In one he said his chickens live in "a house that's just chicken heaven,"in the other that "it takes a tough man to raise a tender chicken." If the former cannot be condemned as deceitful or the latter truthful but offensive (it must indeed take a tough man), they must be unintelligible to the uninitiated.

The newsprint presented their typical distortions of redundant reality. Long Island's *Newsday* had two ads which contribute to the subterfuge with which flesh shops embellish their products. One from a market depicted a cartoon bull with a hat on his head, a flower in his mouth, and a big smile on his friendly face as might remind us of Ferdinand from the classic children's story. In fact, the company's name is Ferdinando's Meats. His is the same disposition of all the animals in the AMI ads: glad to die that others might live. Or so we are led to believe. The second ad went further, and was for a restaurant called Harvest House. The animals were shown offering themselves; advertising its chicken dinner, a chicken proudly serves a platter of what must be the chicken dinner, adding new meaning to the expression "Serve yourself"; promoting its fish dinner, a fish with a spoon in its fin awaits a second helping of, no doubt, more fish dinner; endorsing its veal steak is not a young calf but a young boy, bringing us right back to the cannibalistic connection of young children wishing they were wieners. The second newspaper, *The New York Times*, carried a full-page announcement from a restaurant which equated carnivorism, alcoholism and patriotism. "With unflagging devotion to Steak, Booze, and Old Glory, so proudly we hail: The United States Steakhouse Company."

Enough. The day will come when a future generation views attitudes such as these with the same disdain as our present generation views those of slavery and Nazism. Meanwhile, are murderers and torturers to be trusted with a nation's conscience? Is it such a big step from looking at an animal and seeing only meat and money, to looking at a human and thinking only of pleasure and profit?

America's surviving contacts with animals, besides the spotted dog or black cat or goldfish, are those begun by a knife and ended by a napkin. In 1972, when the country's carnivorous population numbered 200 million, the animals slain in our slaughterhouses ran into or over thirty-six million cattle, three million calves, ten million sheep and lambs, eighty-five million hogs, and three *billion* chickens. In other words, an average American "contacted" fifteen animals a year, and all this disregards the billions of fish, sea animals, and wild animals annually brought to death outside the slaughterhouse.

Calculation of the millions of animals killed within Chicago's

Union Stockyards during its hundred year history would total a number so huge that the real horror would remain incomprehensible. Who knows what even a million is? We should ponder a smaller figure: the hogs alone killed in one single record-breaking day in 1924—123,000. Perhaps we could count that far in one day. Surely we would not fall asleep, as though we were counting sheep.

10. An Apologetic Addendum: Some Second, and Secondary, Thoughts

For the great majority of people a kind of training everywhere takes the place of culture. It is achieved by example, by custom and the very early and firm impression of certain concepts, before any experience, understanding, and power of judgment existed to disturb the work. Thus ideas are implanted which afterwards cling so firmly and are not to be shaken by any instruction just as if they were innate, and they have often been regarded as such, even by philosophers. In this way we can with equal effort impress people with what is right and rational, or with what is most absurd. For example . . . we can accustom them to renounce all animal food, as in Hindustan, or to devour the still warm and quivering pieces cut out from the living animal, as in Abyssinia; to eat human beings as in New Zealand, or to sacrifice their children to Moloch, to castrate themselves, to fling themselves voluntarily on the funeral pile of the deceased—in a word, to do anything we wish.

ARTHUR SCHOPENHAUER
The World as Will and Representation,
Vol. II, Chapter VI, ''On the Doctrine
of Abstract Knowledge, or Knowledge
of Reason''

Muslims and Jews are forbidden to eat pigs, camels, toads, scorpions, and centipedes. The pig taboo is shared also by Jakuts, Malagasy, and Lapps. Fowl is forbidden food to Mongols and Guianas; beef to Hindus and Parsi; hare to Chinese; eggs to Waganda, Bahune, and Caribbees; milk to Dyaks, Malayas, Dravidians, and Ashanti; fish to Zulus; humans to almost all humans; and all the above are forbidden foods to all strict vegetarians. Ancient Greeks, Romans and Aztecs ate dogs; but modern Americans are charged with cruelty to animals if they do.

Sanctions against one kind of flesh food exist only for consumers of other kinds. Anti-cannibalistic instincts apply only to carnivores and are strongest in those who are the srongest carnivores. Carnivores generally do not eat other carnivores: if a lion could eat a tiger, a lion could eat a lion. Cultures that ate dogs were only sporadic carnivores, and their dogs were given even less flesh to eat than they gave themselves dogs to eat.

Just as carnivorous humans never grew claws and fangs, and instead invented knives and spears, neither did they develop instincts to inhibit use of those weapons against other humans. Instead they wrote laws easily ignored and frequently forgotten. "No matter how many laws they passed increasing the severity of the punishments inflicted on those who ate meat in secret," wrote Samuel Butler in *Erewhon*, "the people found means of setting them aside as fast as they were made."

In 1857 in India, a rifle was introduced whose greased cartridges had to be bitten off before loading. Rumors passed through the ranks of the Hindu and Muslim sepoys that the lubricant was either cow or pig fat. To a Hindu, licking the fat of the sacred cow is an unpardonable sin; to a Muslim, tasting the fat of the desecrated pig is an insufferable pollution. Deep social injustice made inevitable the Indian Mutiny against the British, but it was the coating on the cartridges which instigated it.

During the sixth century B.C. in India, Brahmin priests demanded more and more cattle for sacrifice. The drain on the communities' milk animals became intolerable; in revolt against this and other social and religious impositions, a heretic arose. About the same age as Christ would have been when he began his ministry, this Indian leader began preaching for an end to animal slaughter of all kinds. So influential was his campaign that a whole new religion arose around him, and a half a millennium later, around the time of the birth of Christ, even the Brahmin priests of the old religion ceased sacrifices. The name of that rebellious prophet was Buddha.

Buddha could rightfully preach, because he was awake amid a race of somnambulists. But *my* right is rather doubtful. I only guess at the difference between truth and falsehood; I hardly know right from wrong; I see the distinction between only some good and not all evil; I know next to nothing about love and less than that about hate; but I do clearly perceive the faint nuances between the important and the unimportant. For instance, I do know that whether one is wise or otherwise, it is important to consider the differences between truth and falsehood, right and wrong, good and evil, and love and hate. And I do know that if I profess to love animals, then it is right and good and important that I not kill them—though I barely know the difference between life and death.

Perhaps my condemnatory rhetoric has given the impression that I hate people who kill animals, since I love animals. But I do not hate animals that kill animals, and besides, people are animals too. The portions of this discourse directed to carnivores were intended as incentive, not insult. Some of my best friends are carnivores. The butcher is every bit as nice a person as the baker (who uses lard) and the candlestick-maker (who uses tallow). I have made friends of the birds and squirrels, and of the cats that chase them. And while I play with a cat as a squirrel in the tree looks on, I hope the squirrel holds no grudge against me. Likewise with people: as I circulate leaflets in front of his store, I hope the butcher holds no grudge against me.

It is true that because of my vehement and sometimes vengeful voice, I make enemies of strangers and strangers of friends. Love is wonderful, but love sometimes is not enough. Had I never moved to action, no one would have mistaken my devotion to one cause as contempt for its opposites. Hate and murder are evils, but what about hate of murder?

Despite all the evil in the world, I do not know any evil people. But I do know a lot of unhappy people. Ethical philosophies have equated virtue with happiness; more modern ones equate virtue as a means to happiness. Old or new, is vegetarianism virtuous? It certainly is no evil. If virtue comprises happiness and if vegetarianism is virtuous, then vegetarianism is happiness. And is vegetarianism healthful? It certainly is not carcinogenic. If health comprises happiness and if vegetarianism is a means to health, then vegetarianism is a means to happiness. Whether in the cause of the humane or the human, whether we do not eat flesh because we do not kill or we do not kill because we do not eat flesh, the effects are identical. To the moralist, vegetarianism *is* virtuous; to the nutritionist, vegetarianism *is* healthful.

It is no coincidence that what is harmful to the animal killed and grilled is also unhealthy to the killer and griller. Were it opposite, vegetarianism would be no issue and this whole discussion would have come to empty erudition. No doubt would have arisen to be answered, no heresy to be refuted. But this is not the case. Vegetarianism is both a physical relief and a metaphysical reward.

Yet we have our exceptions, those who care about animals but not about themselves (as though they were not animals), those who, as Seneca said, kill themselves with their teeth. These are the ethically minded vegetarians who exhibit their convictions with pins on their lapels but betray the cause by the livid look on their faces. They do not drink blood, but do drink coffee, Coke and Coors. (And is it any less revolting to eat soybeans that have been texturized to taste like flesh than it would be ridiculous to eat flesh that has been transformed to taste like soybeans?) First we must assure our well-being, and proceed from there. Then there are those who do assure their well-being, but proceed nowhere. They are the nutritionally minded vegetarians who care everything about themselves and nothing about the animals. Let no one make the mistake through their example that vegetarianism is a philosophy only of the gut.

Our Western vegetarianism is but one small aspect of a much larger Eastern ideal: ahimsa, complete harmlessness. Upon this ideal alone, I have not hesitated to pronounce ex cathedra judgments on Western society and have refuted the sacred texts of Western religion. Yet I have no intent of fostering Judaic, Christian, or Islamic apostasy solely due to vegetarian tenets. For who am I to judge? For who am I?

I use no cosmetics or pharmaceuticals made from or tested on animals, but that is because I use no cosmetics or pharmaceuticals at all. Unless a fanatic member of the National Rifle Association shoots me in the back or a hired assassin of the American Meat Institute slits my throat, in good health I will live to 101; but then, when I am 102, and a doctor tells me I must take ox bile cortisone or die, I cannot now say what I will do.

I wear canvas shoes spring through fall, plastic shoes fall through spring, no shoes in the middle of the summer, but leather shoes in the middle of the winter. I have no regrets about my leather wallet, since I found it in the gutter. But I must confess that my Macy's monk frock is made of wool.

I switched from oil paints to acrylics so that I might use nylon brushes, not bristle, camel, or sable; but photographic film is coated with gelatin, and anyone would surely shudder who knew the endless exposures of film which I shoot and then simply throw away.

I refuse to patronize any circuses, rodeos, or horse or dog races since their techniques of training are cruel; but it is only the admission fees which keep me away from the equally inhumane zoos. Yet I visit museums of natural history. (Which is worse: stuffing dead animals with cotton, or stuffing live animals into cages?) And I harbor a now not so secret desire to see a bullfight, just once, to prove to myself what I already know—that the Mexican audience in the arena is neither more nor less sadistic than the boxing fans over the one border or the hockey fans over the other.

I bathe and wash with only Kosher soaps (labeled "K" or "U") made from vegetable oils, and brush my teeth with baking soda instead of toothpaste made partially from animal bones; but the charcoal filter for my drinking water is made solely from animal bones.

I avoid killing insects where possible, though I do kill the cockroaches in my indoor garden and did kill the aphids in my garden outdoors. Now that I no longer have a garden outdoors, I let the farmer kill them for me. But I will probably always have to contend with cockroaches, so do not kill the spiders in my bedroom in hope that they will kill the cockroaches in my kitchen.

I very sincerely and very slowly attempted to convert my cat into a vegetarian, but after much spoiled food and much lost patience I gave up. After all, she was three years a carnivore, and an American cat at that. This means her mother and her grandmother and her great-grandmother were all fed lots of flesh, as opposed to, say, an Italian cat, whose mamma, nonna and bisnonna were fed mostly pasta. As it is, her diet is down to only one-fifth flesh; thus instead of "Nine Lives," I feed her only two.

I once held a job in an art library where one of my responsibilities was selecting new books. Its classification system was of an older sort, and books on sports were part of the art collection. I unconditionally refused to requisition any books on hunting, fishing, or horseracing, but knowledgably ordered paperbacks on art though they were bound with glues such as Elmer's which came from the bones of Elsies.

Do I suffer from moral hypochondria, or are my self-imposed predicaments real and necessary? Old oil paintings are primed with rabbit-skin glue; tempera paints are made from eggs, and caseins from milk. If "The Slaughtered Ox" were painted on rabbit-skin glue and with sable brushes, that is Rembrandt's choice and not ours. If we blind ourselves to its beauty, we alone lose.

In a society of the flock and the herd, the rational is also the radical.

Radical vegetarianism means abstinence, and a certain degree of obstinance. It is dialectical, but also a little diabolical.

Its course could lead to a substitution of axioms for insights, but such risks must be taken. These pages are *obiter dicta*, not divine judgments; alternatives, not ultimatums. I have merely exercised my right to regard as false, or at least as equivocal, those maxims that guide life and death in this society. If I had transformed every sentence into a question, would that have been more honest? I make no claim to know the absolute truth, but my claim that a vegetarian's claim is generally closer to the truth than that of a carnivore's merely proves the limitations of my experience, not of carnivorism. That many of the writers quoted from or referred to on these pages were vegetarians only proves the provincial nature of what I read, not the ubiquity of vegetarianism.

Convictions are easily refuted but proved with difficulty. Refutation of one thing—such as carnivorism—is not proof of its opposite—such as vegetarianism. Though it might have been preferable, it was impossible to have spoken of vegetarianism without ever mentioning carnivorism. If boldy outspoken vegetarians become obnoxious, and if carnivores become offended, the losses of social acceptance for the one and of shaky complacence for the other are small costs to exchange for an animal's only life. Expressing love is not enough; we must also express opinions. If feeling are fully expressed by us on one side, feelings will have to be hurt on the other. Neither prince nor pals should infringe upon our principles. Our bodies are our temples: dare we mind our manners, but not our manors?

Carnivores should be asked to expose themselves to the vegetarian dialectic of diet and ethic for one day, for just one day. Since vegetarians are forcibly exposed to the opposite each and every day, that is not much to ask. Some things are easier done than said; once inclination is felt, no more need be said. But, if, after that single day carnivores feel no such inclination to adopt our diet, then we have done all we can do. Waiting on the edge of time, watching for the dawn of that day, that one day, we need not aim to regain the whole of the Garden of Eden: the Tree of Life is enough. That tree, mentioned in only the first and last books of the Bible, is the symbol both of time's beginning and eternity's end.

Meanwhile, until that day, what can we do? Catholics and Jews, Blacks and Reds, Chicanos and Indians, gays and women, all in their time have demanded their rights as Americans, and all have gotten or are on their way to getting them. But no group of animals is able to petition Congress to protect their rights as animals. Both that petition and protection rest with you and me. According to Kant's moral postulate "You can because you ought."

Though neither an Amos nor a Hosea, a Jeremiah nor an Isaiah, I sense others' revulsion along with my own against injustices embedded in our society, and as much for them as for myself I have spoken. Let no one accuse me of acquiescence and self-glossotomy. Let no one say of me:

Like a lamb that is led to the slaughter
and like a sheep that before its shearers is dumb,
so he opened not his mouth.

Thus this had to be written: not as a voice of sanity amid so much madness—for the distinction is moot and easy to refute—-but as a voice of the living amid the silence of the dead.

Posthumous Postscript

Edgar Kupfer, born in 1906 in Koberwitz near Breslau, was a pacifist. Imprisoned in 1940 in Dachau, he was blessed either by the gods or by the guards two years later with a clerical job in the concentration camp storeroom. On stolen scraps of paper and with pieces of pencil, he stealthily scribbled a secret diary. For the next three years he buried his writings, an idea no doubt inspired from burying the dead. On April 29, 1945, Dachau was liberated; Edgar Kupfer was freed.

The *Dachau Diaries* too were freed, and published in 1956. By this time Kupfer-Koberwitz had moved to Chicago, where he lived a St. Stephen's stone's throw from the Union Stockyards. From his Dachau notes kept prior to and shortly after the liberation, he wrote an essay on vegetarianism subsequently translated into immigrant English. A carbon copy of the original 38-page typescript from which the following pages are excerpted, along with the four boxes containing the original *Dachau Diaries*, are now preserved in the Special Collection of the Library of the University of Chicago, ironically the same university which formerly housed the Research Laboratories of the American Meat Institute.

As far as can be determined, this marks the first publication in a book of even these few passages selected from the whole, either in German or in English. Special thanks is due to the librarians of the Special Collection, without whose help both the manuscript and the shroud surrounding it would never have been known. Permission to publish these segments was sought from all those involved in the donation of "Animals, My Brethren" to the University. But, alas, they have died, or have been forgotten by others, or have themselves forgotten.

"Animals, My Brethren"
by Edgar Kupfer-Koberwitz

The following pages were written in the Concentration Camp Dachau, in the midst of all kinds of cruelties. They were furtively scrawled in a hospital barrack where I stayed during my illness, in a time when Death grasped day by day after us, when we lost twelve thousand within four and a half months.

Dear Friend:

You asked me why I do not eat meat and you are wondering at the reasons of my behavior. Perhaps you think I took a vow—some kind of penitence—denying me all the glorious pleasures of eating meat. You remember juicy steaks, succulent fishes, wonderfully tasted sauces, deliciously smoked ham and thousand wonders prepared out of meat, charming thousands of human palates; certainly you will remember the delicacy of roasted chicken. Now, you see, I am refusing all these pleasures and you think that only penitence, or a solemn vow, a great sacrifice could deny me that manner of enjoying life, induce me to endure a great resignment.

* * *

You look astonished, you ask the question: "But why and what for?" And you are wondering that you nearly guessed the very reason. But if I am, now, trying to explain you the very reason in one concise sentence, you will be astonished once more how far your guessing had been from my real motive. Listen to what I have to tell you:

I refuse to eat animals because I cannot nourish myself by the sufferings and by the death of other creatures. I refuse to do so, because I suffered so painfully myself that I can feel the pains of others by recalling my own sufferings.

I feel happy, nobody persecutes me; why should I persecute other beings or cause them to be persecuted?

I feel happy, I am no prisoner, I am free; why should I cause other creatures to be made prisoners and thrown into jail?

I feel happy, nobody harms me; why should I harm other creatures or have them harmed?

133

I feel happy, nobody wounds me; nobody kills me; why should I wound or kill other creatures or cause them to be wounded or killed for my pleasure and convenience?

Is it not only too natural that I do not inflict on other creatures the same thing which, I hope and fear, will never be inflicted on me? Would it not be most unfair to do such things for no other purpose than for enjoying a trifling physical pleasure at the expense of others' sufferings, others' deaths?

These creatures are smaller and more helpless than I am, but can you imagine a reasonable man of noble feelings who would like to base on such a difference a claim or right to abuse the weakness and the smallness of others? Don't you think that it is just the bigger, the stronger, the superior's duty to protect the weaker creatures instead of persecuting them, instead of killing them? "Noblesse oblige." I want to act in a noble way.

* * *

I recall the horrible epoch of inquisition and I am sorry to state that the time of tribunals for heretics has not yet passed by, that day by day, men use to cook in boiling water other creatures which are helplessly given in the hands of their torturers. I am horrified by the idea that such men are civilized people, no rough barbarians, no natives. But in spite of all, they are only primitively civilized, primitively adapted to their cultural environment. The average European, flowing over with highbrow ideas and beautiful speeches, commits all kinds of cruelties, smilingly, not because he is compelled to do so, but because he wants to do so. Not because he lacks the faculty to reflect upon and to realize all the dreadful things they are performing. Oh no! Only because they do not want to see the facts. Otherwise they would be troubled and worried in their pleasures.

* * *

It is quite natural what people are telling you. How could they do otherwise? I hear them telling about experiences, about utilities, and I know that they consider certain acts related to slaughtering as unavoidable. Perhaps they succeeded to win you over. I guess that from your letter.

Still, considering the necessities only, one might, perhaps, agree with such people. But is there really such a necessity? The thesis may be contested. Perhaps there exists still some kind of necessity for such persons who have not yet developed into full conscious personalities.

I am not preaching to them. I am writing this letter to you, to an already awakened individual who rationally controls his impulses, who feels responsible—internally and externally—of his acts, who knows that our supreme court is sitting in our conscience. There is no appellate jurisdiction against it.

Is there any necessity by which a fully self-conscious man can be induced to slaughter? In the affirmative, each individual may have the courage to do it by his own hands. It is, evidently, a miserable kind of cowardice to pay other people to perform the blood-stained job, from which the normal man refrains in horror and dismay. Such servants are given some farthings for their bloody work, and one buys from them the desired parts of the killed animal—if possible prepared in such a way that it does not any more recall the discomfortable circumstances, nor the animal, nor its being killed, nor the bloodshed.

* * *

I think that men will be killed and tortured as long as animals are killed and tortured. So long there will be wars too. Because killing must be trained and perfected on smaller objects, morally and technically.

I see no reason to feel outraged by what others are doing, neither by the great nor by the smaller acts of violence and cruelty. But, I think, it is high time to feel outraged by all the small and great acts of violence and cruelty which we perform ourselves. And because it is much easier to win the smaller battles than the big ones, I think we should try to get over first our own trends towards smaller violence and cruelty, to avoid, or better, to overcome them once and for all. Then the day will come when it will be easy for us to fight and to overcome even the great cruelties. But we are still sleeping, all of us, in habitudes and inherited attitudes. They are like a fat, juicy sauce which helps us to swallow our own cruelties without tasting their bitterness.

I have not the intention to point out with my finger at this and that, at definite persons and definite situations. I think it is much more my duty to stir up my own conscience in smaller matters, to try to understand other people better, to get better and less selfish. Why should it be impossible then to act accordingly with regard to more important issues?

That is the point: I want to grow up into a better world where a higher law grants more happiness, in a new world where God's commandment reigns:

You Shall Love Each Other

References

To a man whose mind is free there is something even more intolerable in the sufferings of animals than in the sufferings of man. For with the latter it is at least admitted that suffering is evil and that the man who causes it is a criminal. But thousands of animals are uselessly butchered every day without a shadow of remorse. If any man were to refer to it, he would be thought ridiculous. —And that is the unpardonable crime. That alone is the justification of all that men may suffer.

ROMAIN ROLLAND
Jean-Christophe: Journey's End,
a section shortly before "The
New Dawn"

The vegetarian among carnivores sometimes eats alone, and might be thought ridiculous for it. In the bodily sense the solitude is quite definite: not even a cow or fish or chicken shares the table. But in the spiritual sense the prose of philosophers and the praise of poets accompany the meal along with the blessings of the cow and fish and chicken and the silent perfect egg. Those statements of sentiment which have prefaced or unifed these chapters are by no means exhausted and were limited in number only by the chapters themselves. The works from which they **were** drawn are commonly called classics, so no extensive description of them is needed here. New editions are issued almost every decade, and the few no longer in print can be found in most university libraries.

In addition to the Bible, (The Revised Standard Version), these honorable authors and their works were quoted.

Bibliography One

1. Blake, "Auguries of Innocence"
2. Brecht, "Writing the Truth: Five Difficulties"
3. Butler, *Erewhon*
4. Ibsen, *Enemy of the People*
5. Kafka, "Investigations of a Dog"
6. Nietzsche, *The Gay Science* and *The Genealogy of Morals*

 7. Pasolini, ''A Desperate Vitality''.
 8. Plato, *Crito* and *Theaetetus*
 9. Plutarch, ''The Eating of Meat''
10. Porphyry, *On Abstinence from Animal Food*
11. Rolland, *Jean-Christophe*
12. Schopenhauer, *On the Basis of Morality, Parerga and Paralipomena*, and *The World as Will and Representation*
13. Schweitzer, *Reverence for Life*
14. Mary Shelley, *Frankenstein*
15. Percy Shelley, ''A Vindication of Natural Diet''
16. Steiner, ''Problems of Nutrition''
17. Tolstoy, ''The First Step''
18. Voltaire, *Candide*

Nearly half of these authors were not themselves vegetarians, but one need not be a vegetarian to recognize its merits and to join in the ideological battle. Vegetarian or not, such a dossier as the above is more useful in constructing a case for prosecution than in conducting a scholarly investigation of a serious subject. For the latter we must turn from the philosophers and poets to the polemicists.

Three books published during the 1970s remain our essential ethical treatises which supplement each other and together complement this book:

Bibliography Two

1. Tom Regan and Peter Singer, *Animal Rights and Human Obligations* (Englewood Cliffs, NJ: Prentice Hall, 1976).
2. Peter Singer, *Animal Liberation: A New Ethics for Our Treatment of Animals* (New York: New York Review of Books, 1975).
3. Stephen Clark, *The Moral Status of Animals* (Oxford: Clarendon Press, 1977).

The above authors cited were all concerned with ethics and, except for Shelley, nearly totally disregarded diet. The following books are just the opposite, that is concerned with diet, almost absolutely ignoring ethics. These are sometimes hard to locate, but usually can be ordered through the local health food store. They are listed in the order as found in the second chapter and aligned with each step:

Bibliography Three

1. Frances Moore Lappé, *Diet for a Small Planet* (New York: Ballantine Books, 1971).

2. Paavo Airola, *Are You Confused?* (Phoenix: Health Plus, 1971) and *How to Get Well* (Phoenix: Health Plus, 1974).

3. Kathy Dinaburg and D'Ann Akel, *Nutrition Survival Kit* (Los Angeles: Panjandrum Books, 1976).

4. George Ohsawa and Herman Aihara, *Macrobiotics: An Invitation to Health and Happiness* (1971) and a catalog of other macrobiotic literature are available from the George Ohsawa Macrobiotic Foundation, 1471 10th Avenue, San Francisco, CA 94122.

5. Paul Bragg, *The Miracle of Fasting*. All his books and their catalog are available from Health Science, Box 477, Hot Springs, CA 92240.

6. Herbert Shelton, *Health for the Millions* (1968), *Fasting for the Renewal of Life* (1977), and all Natural Hygienic works, including William Esser's *Dictionary of Man's Foods* (1972), and a catalog of the literature are available from the American Natural Hygiene Society, Box 30630, Tampa, FL 33630.

7. Viktoras Kulvinskas, *Survival into the 21st Century: Planetary Healers Manual* (1975) and a catalog of related raw food and fruitarian literature are available from 21st Century Publications, Box 702, Fairfield, IA 52556.

8. Arnold Ehret, *Mucusless Diet Healing System* (1922), other Ehret works, and a catalog of other fruitarian literature are available from the Ehret LIterature Publishing Company, Beaumont, CA 92223.

After diet and after ethics, eventually we might tire of the dialectical and wish to attend as well to the delectable. Cookbooks and raw recipe books which exclude the use of all flesh, fish, milk and eggs are becoming abundant. The three best cookbooks are followed by the three best raw recipe books:

Bibliography Four

1. Edyth Cottrell, *Oats, Peas, Beans and Barley* (Santa Barbara, CA: Woodbridge Press, 1974).

*2. Frank and Rosalie Hurd, *Ten Talents* (1968), available from their home in Chisholm, Minnesota.

3. Jethro Kloss, *Back to Eden Cookbook* (Santa Barbara, CA: Woodbridge Press, 1974).

4. Marcia Acciardo, *Light Eating for Survival* (Wethersfield, CT: Omangod Press, 1977).

5. Elizabeth and Elton Baker, *The UNcook Book* (Saguache, CO: Communication Creativity, 1981).

6. Ann Wigmore, *Recipes for Life* (Boston: Rising Sun Publishers, 1978).

Next we must consider the books that will never be written, the books by authors too busily engaged in the vegetarian activist movement to find time to put page-by-page into words what day-by-day they put into action. Or, if they do write, it is more to be right than to be read. Often the persons about whom we speak affix their names to very loosely formed not-for-profit organizations, yet they and their equally under or unpaid and unrecognized spouses remain the only staff. Their efforts must not be confused with those influential wildlife federations which camouflage hunting gangs, nor even with those traditional vegetarian social clubs concerned only with picnics and potluck dinners. And, unlike those who parade live calves through McDonald's restaurants or liberate caged dolphins into the sea or fast on fruit juice in front of three network television cameras, they avoid the dramatic. Their work, confined within four walls of their offices, instead borders on the dreary; they circulate petitions and pleas, they book public service announcements, they take and make phone calls and, most important, they answer the repetitive questions of a thousand daily supplicants such as ourselves, people they will never meet. We, with more time than we could ever usefully fill or more money than we deserve, might consider donating one or the other to them who have enough of neither. Singling out three activist groups is not done to exclude the others, but these are three to which the author's own testimony can vouch; the dedication of the workers and the worthiness of their cause is commendable indeed.

Bibliography Five

1. *American Vegetarians*, Box 1155, Akron, OH 44309. Phone: (216) 535-4583.
2. *Trans-Species Unlimited*, Box 1553, Williamsport, PA 17703. Phone: (717) 322-3252.
3. *Farm Sanctuary*, Box 37, Rockland, DE 19732. Phone: (302) 654-9026.

After tables of contents we must read lists of ingredients. Recognizing that our doctrines govern the interiors as much of bedroom closets and bathroom cabinets as of refrigerators and sprout jars, a small country store located amid Georgia peanut plantations caters to our needs. Clothing and toiletries traditionally manufactured from the bodies of our animal buddies here congregate under one roof for a vegetarian potluck dinner. And because the business is mail-order we can invite individual items under our roofs too. It carries nylon wallets and paper purses, rubber shoes and cotton belts, vegetable oil soaps and animal test-free cosmetics, and toothpastes made of chalk or clay instead of bone or urine. The store also stocks a small selection of books. Although bound in bone glue, their subject matter is vegetarian.

Bibliography Six

Amberwood, 125 Shoal Creek Road, Fayetteville, GA 30214. Phone: (404) 461-8578.

Last, the novice might seek a book which is a digest of all the reasons for vegetarianism, which includes recipes along with homilies, which repeats histories while it deletes mysteries, and which provides facts in milligrams and figures in diagrams. Three examples of such a book are:

Bibliography Seven

1. Nat Altman, *Eating for Life* (Wheaton, IL: Theosophical Publishing House, 1977).
2. Dudley Giehl, *Vegetarianism: A Way of Life* (New York: Harper & Row, 1979).
3. Vic Sussman, *The Vegetarian Alternative* (Emmaus, PA: Rodale Books, 1978).

Had these authors not written their books, this author would have had to have done it. As it is, they were written; thus our book at hand either disregarded or assumed the fat facts, and was able to proceed to slim logic—indeed at times mad logic.

OTHER BOOKS OF INTEREST FROM
PANJANDRUM BOOKS

Nutrition Survival Kit by Kathy Dinaburg and D'Ann Akel, R.D. ($6.95 pap., $12.00 cl.)
The most concise and lively synthesis yet of advanced nutrition information and mouth-watering natural foods recipes (over 200), hints and resources. Recommended by *Let's Live, Vegetarian Times, Nutrition Health Review, Not Man Apart.*

Kitchen Cosmetics by Jeanne Rose. Using Herbs, Fruits and Eatables in Natural Cosmetics. ($5.95 pap., $9.95 cl.)
One of America's best known herbalists presents recipes and formulas for the hair, hands, legs, feet and face using common kitchen and garden herbs (and some not so common), flowers and fruit. Original line drawings.

Fruits & Sprouts: Radical Vegetarian Recipes by Mark Mathew Braunstein. ($7.95 pap., *forthcoming*)
The author of *Radical Vegetarianism* combines theory with practice and presents fruit breakfasts and sprout suppers. Also includes complete instructions on how to grow more than 30 varieties of sprouts and how to select more than 30 varieties of fruits. Many recipes.

Palm Leaf Patterns: A New Approach to Clothing Design by Margaret Fisher. ($5.95 pap.)
The book itself is a full-scale four-color pattern for making a pair of loose-fitting, drawstring pants. Also discussion of relationship between clothing and health.

The Famous Vegetarian Cookbook: The Lives, Recipes, and Portraits of the World's Great Vegetarians by Rynn Berry. ($7.95 pap. $15.95 cloth, Oct. '83)
Here is a pot-pourri of biographical profiles, pencil portraits, and almost 100 recipes that go to make up a lively, informal history of vegetarianism from antiquity to the present. Includes da Vinci, Shelley, Tolstoy, Paul and Linda McCartney, Marty Feldman, I.B. Singer and many others. In all, a literary, historical, and culinary delight.

Four Seasons Cookbook by Helen Gershen et. al. ($7.95 pap.
$14.95 cloth)

Containing over 100 time-tested recipes and suggested
menus, this hand-calligraphed cookbook is composed of
four seasonal sections, each season of the year having its
distinctive menus and recipes. Appetizers include Tomatoes Lutece, and Cool Cream of Cucumber Soup; main
dishes, Quiche and Broccoli Casserole; desserts, Easy Egg-
nog Cake and Pumpkin Cheese Cake. Although not exclu
sively a vegetarian cookbook, all those with demanding
palates will be pleased.